JUST DO!

Stories about **DISCOVERING PURPOSE,**
GAINING PERSPECTIVE and **BEING PRESENT.**

JUST DO!

Stories about DISCOVERING PURPOSE, GAINING PERSPECTIVE and BEING PRESENT.

BRANDON JANOUS

BJ BOOKS
Knoxville, TN
Nashville, TN

Published by BJ Books

First printing, December 2022

Library of Congress Cataloging-In-Publication Data
Janous, Brandon
    JUST DO!: Stories about Discovering Purpose, Gaining Perspective, and Being Present.
    Brandon Janous - 1st ed.
    p. cm.
    Includes bibliographical references.
    ISBN 9798218069582
    1. Inspiration 2. Family 3. Religion

Cover Design by Tim Marshall, Nashville, TN
RV Art by iralu - Kharkiv, Ukraine
Printed in China

Rach, thank you so much for choosing me. And though I'd planned to spend the rest of my life with you, thank you for spending the rest of yours with me. You are the best thing...

CONTENTS

FOREWORD

I remember a few years ago, we were on a family vacation. We all know that taking pictures of a special trip like that is a must because we desire to capture a snapshot of a memory. As we were a couple days into our wonderful and memorable experience together, I looked at everyone. We all had our phones out and were either filming or taking a photo of the breathtaking sunset. And I thought to myself, are we really "experiencing" the moment or just trying to capture a mere portrait of it. So I told everyone: "Let's put our phones down and enjoy God's beautiful display in front of us. Let's really soak in the moment."

That experience gave me a new perspective on things. I made it my mission to create memories and relish every opportunity to be with my family.

In *Just Do!*, Brandon does just that. He takes us on a journey of his own experience of creating those memories for his own family.

With a raw look at this adventure, you'll find so much joy in hearing the amazing stories of a father who understands the importance of family - learning to truly connect, living life to the fullest, and understanding what it means to be truly present.

One of my favorite things about Brandon is his honesty about his mistakes and shortcomings. Still, instead of walking in shame, he gives us a sneak peek into the lessons he gleaned from those time s.

As you learn about his wife Rachel, the life she lived, and the way she loved, you'll understand the joy, spunk, and life she brought wherever she went.

Buckle up and get some snacks for your journey through this heartwarming and exciting adventure of a family making some of the most incredible memories that will last a lifetime. Hopefully this book will inspire you, as it did me, to "Just Do."

Jeremy Camp
GRAMMY®-nominated Singer/Songwriter

PROLOGUE

On March 1, 2020, my wife, Rachel, took her last breath here on earth and went to dance with Jesus in Heaven. I just know He was awaiting her arrival with arms wide open and a big ol' smile on His face. And I'm certain that as they embraced, He whispered in her ear, "Well done, Rachel, well done."

She fought so hard. She gave it everything she had. And everything she had was so dang much.

But on that day, March 1, 2020, at 4:30-something p.m., Rachel won the race and received her crown.

My plan was to spend the rest of my life with Rachel, and though that's not how it happened, I'm honored that she spent the rest of her life with me.

I met Rachel when I was twenty, and I knew the moment I laid eyes on her that no one could ever love her more than I would.

After a long and hard chase, I somehow talked her into marrying me, and I knew at that moment that no one could ever love her more than I would.

We had three precious babies, Hadley, Cooper, and Macklin, and each time I got to watch her become "mommy" again, I was certain that no one could ever love her more than I would.

We got diagnosed with cancer on April 17, 2018, and as each day went by and I watched her continue to fight for her life, I fell harder and harder for her. I had zero doubt that there was anyone else on the planet that could love her more than I would.

I'll never forget the moment she left us for her eternal home. As I sat in that chair, right next to her hospital bed, tears rolling down my face, with her hand in mine, watching her rest in such peace, I couldn't help but smile, knowing that for the first time in a very long time, Rachel had no more pain. She would suffer no more. She would cry no more tears. There would be no more doctors' appointments. There would be no more treatment plans.

There would be no more uncertainty. She didn't have to worry about anything anymore. Because on that day, Rachel beat cancer for good.

And as hard as that day was, and as hard as the following days were going to be, I took joy in the fact that on March 1, 2020, at 4:30-something p.m., Rachel was finally in the arms of the only one that would love her more than I ever could.

INTRODUCTION

This wasn't how I'd expected my first book to begin. To be honest, before Rachel got sick, I'd already written much of what you'll read if you keep going. And for the most part, it's not sad. I had no intention of making you cry or bringing you to tears. Actually, what I'd written before cancer was fun, exciting, joyful, funny, and all the other feel-good words. But then life happened.

Life has a way of doing that. It just happens.

It would be easy for you to read that opening passage and think that you've stumbled upon a book full of pain and sorrow. But I'm here to assure you that what you'll find in the following pages isn't that. Yes, we lost Rachel. Yes, I'm going to spend some time talking about that season because she deserves to be talked about, and her story deserves to be told. Yes, it's sad and hard and what happened may not make sense most days. But what you're not going to find is a book about death or dying. That's not what this is. That's not what Rachel would have wanted. It's not littered with stories from the hospital or the cancer center. It could be because there were so many beautiful lessons during those days. But that's not what this story is. It's actually quite the opposite. This book is about living. It's about loving. It's about doing. Because that's what Rachel chose to do every single moment of every single day. She lived. She loved. And even as she was dying, she continued to do.

My hope for this book is that through sharing more of our family's stories, you choose to live and love a little differently going forward. Not just for a day or two. But all the days that you have left. And that's not a fairy tale dream because I watched someone live her entire life that way. Her name was Rachel. And in this book, you're invited to hear some more of her story.

And though she is one of the main characters, there are a few other stars as well. They just happen to be our kids: Hadley, Cooper, and Macklin. And they are spectacular. Because Rachel chose me and invited me on the journey of a lifetime, I get to tell her story. I get to tell their story. I get to tell the story of us.

I must warn you. It'll be unedited. It'll be pretty raw. The grammar and punctuation may not be perfect. Wait, I take that back, I can promise you that it will be far from perfect. You may wonder to yourself many times throughout your reading how some of the pages even got approved for print. I used to care about grammar and punctuation and I used to think that you weren't allowed to put a book out there that wasn't edited to perfection. Until I started writing and people started editing and I realized that it didn't sound like me anymore. I was told to hire an editor but if I'm going to tell our story, I need to tell it the way it actually went down, not the way the editors want it to sound like it went down. So I didn't hire an editor.

Don't get me wrong, I love editors. I think they are great. And they are needed for most books. Just not this book. Just not our book. So if you're an English teacher, I'm sorry in advance. If grammar is your thing, I'm so sorry you're going to have to endure the pain that is this book. And if you don't like the words "y'all" or "stinkin," I'm really sorry for what you're about to read.

Oh, and one more thing. The people that told me to hire an editor also told me that I shouldn't put pictures in my book. But I did. I wasn't going to because they told me not to. But then I did. Because, well, you'll see.

That being said, if you'll just bear with me...if you'll give me a ton of grace...if you read this through the eyes of someone who just happened to land upon my Facebook or Instagram page, I think you may just enjoy it. Heck, you may even take something from it. At least I hope that you do.

Also, I need to ask a favor: if you're really going to read this book...if you're truly ready to go on this adventure with us, I need to ask you to make it through the first section. It's not my favorite section and probably won't be yours either. So I just need you to make it to Chapter 7. Can you do that for me?

Now, don't go skipping the first six chapters because there is some really good stuff there and it lays the groundwork for the rest of the book. But in that first section, there is just a lot of "me" and I hate talking about me. The good stuff comes later on. So if you're willing to deal with a little too much "me" at the beginning, I promise the rest of the way, I'll give you what you came here for.

Ok, now that we've gotten that out of the way, before we really get into the pages of the book, I have a confession to make. I'm not an expert. To be honest, I'm so far from even being close to an expert on anything, for that matter. So if you were looking for an expert's guide to discovering purpose, gaining perspective, being present, or being a perfect dad or the best husband, you should probably keep searching. I'm sure there are some great books by some amazing experts on these topics. But I'm just not that person.

I am just a dude that struggles daily to balance all that life throws his way. I struggle with patience. I struggle with presence. I struggle with parenting. I get tired. I get overwhelmed. And while we are being honest, most days, just after dinner time, I run out of steam and have nothing left to give. I struggle. A lot. I suck. A lot. And as long as you're willing to give me some grace, I'm going to be as real and authentic as I can possibly be.

I want to share with you some of the good times because the good times are just that - good. But over the last few years, I've found that some of the greatest stuff comes out of some of the hardest and ugliest times. The times when I was at my worst. You may find yourself hating the person that I was at times. You may find yourself relating to the person that I was at times. But no matter where you find yourself, it's just important to me that I don't sugarcoat any of it and that I always tell it like it was. So as long as you're cool if it gets a little messy and as long as you're willing to forgive all of my shortcomings, then I couldn't be more excited to have you on this journey with me. On this journey with us.

Here is my hope. It's not to impress you (those days are long gone); it's to have some kind of impact on you. It's for you to hear this, read this, however you take it in, and for it to cause you to take action, even if it's a seemingly small action. Or it causes you to make a change, even if it's a seemingly small change. Or it causes you to do. Do something. Do anything. Just do.

I hope this book encourages you. I hope it equips you. I hope by the time you're done reading this book, you'll be better for it. I don't expect a miracle. I'm not in the business of making miracles happen. I leave that to the Big Guy. But I can promise you that you aren't wasting your time by being here. I can promise I'm going to pour all I have to give into the following pages. And that the stories you're about to read are filled with faith, hope, and love. And I don't know about you, but as for me and my house, we are always seeking more of that stuff. Because that's the good stuff.

I do have one request. If, after reading this book, it did anything to make you a better dad, mom, husband, wife, child, boss, co-worker, teammate, or human, would you mind passing it on to someone else? That would be the ultimate compliment.

Finally, I just want to thank you for being here. According to Google, 129,864,880 books have been published to date. And you chose to read this one. You chose to read the one hundred twenty-nine million eight hundred sixty-four thousand eight hundred and eighty-first book ever written. That's a huge deal, and I'm forever grateful.

So, thank you. Thank you for caring about this story. Thank you for taking the time to read it. Thank you for making it this far with me. Sometimes I don't have the best words, and this just happens to be one of those times because I honestly can't even believe you're here. That being said, I just want to say thank you.

THE
BEGINNING

THE CHASE

It's impossible for me to really dive into where we are today without giving you a little backstory on Rachel and me. A little over 12 years ago, the girl who said, "I do," did an amazing service to the man I am today. I don't know that I ever attained the level of the man that she deserved, but I did try each day to become better for her.

She was the contrast that made our photos seem so lively. She didn't have a selfish bone in her body. No matter what life threw her way, she continued to teach me what it looked like to live a grace-filled life. I'd stand in awe as she taught all those she came into contact with how to celebrate life's imperfections.

From the moment I laid eyes on her, the chase was on. Little did I know at the time just how long it would take me to convince her to marry me. But I'd do it a million times over.

It all started because of flag football. Yep, that's right; if it wasn't for flag football, there would be no us. No Hadley, Cooper, or Macklin. And for sure, no book that you're currently reading.

Let me take you back to the foundation of where this chase actually began. I went to the University of Missouri - MIZ, and I'm a proud Tiger. And I'm so thankful that I went to that school because Mizzou, and the people that I eventually met there, introduced me to a life and a special someone that was beyond my wildest dreams.

During my sophomore year, my buddies and I decided to join a fraternity together. There were five of us in total, and we were all committed to doing the "Greek Life" together. All for one and one for all. We all loved Jesus and hoped to be a light in a sometimes dark Greek system. In addition, we were all pretty good athletes, and the Greek intramural system was the best there was.

When we began our journey, our house wasn't known for its athletics, but we were there to change that. And we did. We made some noise right away and even dethroned the mighty Betas in flag football. The coveted title they had held for many years was yanked out from under them, and if I remember right, we hammered them. We were just better, and it showed. This utter domination on the flag football field allowed us the opportunity to play in a national flag football tournament in Lincoln, Nebraska.

I can tell y'all are super impressed with my athletic accomplishments. Listen, I was too small to play real football. My parents didn't want me to get hurt. So flag football it was. And I'm not even a little ashamed. Ok, maybe a little. But not a lot.

Back to the story.

At that point in my life, I'd never been to Lincoln, Nebraska. Nor had I ever desired to go to Lincoln, Nebraska. Especially not in the middle of November. I wondered why this tournament couldn't have been in San Diego, Miami, or somewhere with a better climate. When we arrived, the weather channel announced a -20°F wind chill. I'm almost positive it didn't get any warmer over the entire weekend. The weather was not the highlight of my weekend. The football was not the highlight of my weekend. I honestly don't even remember how we did. The highlight of my weekend was our hostess.

My fraternity buddies attended high school with a girl named Rachel, who just so happened to be a dancer for the University of Nebraska. Before our trip, they had reached out to her to see if she and her roommates would be willing to host about ten guys for the weekend. I mean, we were broke. So, at the time, the idea of ten guys in a tiny apartment seemed to make the most sense.

Rachel agreed to be our hostess, and little did I know that this particular weekend was about to turn out far differently than I could have ever imagined. Because of flag football, my life would never be the same. On our drive up from Columbia to Lincoln, my buddy Casey started to tease me that I was going to fall for this Rachel girl. I told him that he was crazy. I was there to win some football games, not to flirt with some girl. Plus, why would I want to have any interest in a girl that lived six hours away from me?

"Seems like a really stupid idea to me," I told him.

It wasn't stupid. It wasn't even close to stupid. Casey was so right, and I was about to fall head over heels for this girl. You know how people always talk about those love at first sight moments? Well, I don't know if that was the case, but I do know that the moment she opened the door and I saw her smile, I was done. It was over. Now that I think about it, it absolutely was love at first sight. The football didn't matter. The distance didn't matter. The negative wind chill didn't matter. Nothing else mattered that weekend except learning as much as I could about this Rachel girl.

She was funny. She was beautiful. She was engaging. She was super sweet. She was so much fun to be around. I remember being annoyed that we had to go play football while we were there because I wasn't going to be around Rachel. If I remember right, she did come to one of our games. I think I probably played pretty awesome, so I'm sure she was super impressed. I mean, she was dancing at all the University of Nebraska football games and had a sideline view of all those players. Still, I'm sure my flag football skills really took her admiration for me to another level.

The weekend went by way too quickly, and come Sunday, we were back on the road to Mizzou. I remember Casey looking at me as we pulled away, with an "I told you so" grin on his face. He didn't need to say a word. He knew, and so did I. I just wondered if she did too.

There was no fast track to Rachel and me being together. We would keep in touch here and there for the next ten years. The truth is that I spent the next ten years trying to convince her that she should be with me. We would see each other occasionally, but the timing was never right. She would come to my fraternity formals if she was able to sneak away for a weekend. Once in a while, I'd receive a last-minute invite to a wedding when she couldn't find another date. There were a few other occasions where we would make it a point to connect, but there was never a time where it made sense to really give "us" a try. Whether it was the distance, the timing, or all of the stupid boyfriends she dated before me, it just never seemed to work out for us.

When I lived in Columbia, she was living in Lincoln. When I moved to Tucson after college, she was beginning nursing school in Kansas City. When I decided to take a once-in-a-lifetime opportunity in Hawaii, she was deciding where to start her career, and Hawaii wasn't on the list. It's not like we weren't dating other people during this ten-year chase. I know that she dated a few guys off and on. We never really talked about them, so I'll just assume they were lame. On the contrary, I actually dated some amazing girls, but the problem was that no one was her. I broke up with way too many really cool girls because they weren't Rachel. I always used the "it's not you, it's me" line, but in the end, what I should have said was, "It's not you. You're just not Rachel, so I guess it *is* kind of you."

A few months after I moved to Hawaii, I remember having a conversation with a buddy explaining to him that I'd really like to give this relationship with Rachel a shot. I just needed to know if this was something worth pursuing or if I just needed to let it go for good. So I sent her an email. Listen, this was like 2009, so give me a break. Email was a super strong and probably romantic form of communication.

Anyway, in the email, I laid it all out there. I told her how I was feeling and that I'd felt that way for a really long time. I told her that I was tired of putting it off and that I really wanted to give "us" a shot. Like a real shot. Not a "wedding date because I don't have a date" kind of shot. But like a "let's date and maybe get married" type of shot. I'm sure I said it better than that. I looked for the original email, so I could impress y'all with how awesome I was in my plea. But, it's probably best for all of us that I couldn't find it.

Needless to say, after laying it all out there and putting my heart on the line, I asked her if she would come to Hawaii and see me during her upcoming spring break.

She replied via email with something along the lines of "no."

So, that sucked.

I'm pretty certain it was because she had a boyfriend at the time, but she always denied that. I just knew it had to be that. Why else would she say "no" to a free trip to Hawaii? Whatever the reason, it stung. Bad.

And honestly, I took the "no" as just that. A firm, hard, not a chance "no." And I was finally willing to close the door after a long, hard-fought, ten-year chase. I'd finally admitted to myself that it was time to move on. It's not that I wanted to give up, but I'd prayed so much about her over the years, and this time I took the "no" as not just coming from Rachel, but I thought maybe this time God was saying, "not a chance, kid." And it sucked.

I didn't respond to her "no" email right away because I just didn't know how to say what I wanted to say. So, I said nothing.

I knew that eventually I would need to respond, but all I could think to say was, "well, that sucks," and I just wasn't sure that's how I wanted it to go. Thankfully, before I had the chance to send her my "that sucks" reply, I got a follow-up email. She had a sudden change of heart and now wanted to come to Hawaii.

She now wanted to come see me. Or maybe it was just Hawaii she wanted to see, but it didn't matter because all that mattered was that she was coming.

I was tempted to just reply "no," but that was my pride sneaking in, and that would have been really stupid. So I didn't do that. My immediate thought was that she must have just dumped her boyfriend - the one she said she didn't have. But the truth is that I didn't care why she had changed her mind. I didn't care what the circumstances were that led her to that decision...I was just thrilled. She would be visiting me in Hawaii a few weeks later, and we would spend the longest consecutive time together that we'd ever had: 72 whole hours.

We made it very clear to each other that there would be no expectations. We even named our 72 hours together - "Spring Break 2009 - No Expectations." I wanted to get t-shirts made, but then there would have been expectations. That would have gone against the goal of not having expectations. I won't get into all the details of the 72 hours we had together, but I will tell you this: 48 hours after she arrived, we had pretty much planned the wedding.

Fast forward three months later, and I was having breakfast with her dad asking for his daughter's hand in marriage. The next night I proposed to her in front of all our family and friends. I got a little nervous before popping the question because earlier that day we received the news that Michael Jackson had died. Rachel loved her some MJ. We joked for many years that his passing and my proposal is why that day had become known as the worst day and the best day of her life. Eight months later, on March 13, 2010, after a ten-year chase, the chase was conclusively over because that was the day when she finally said, "I do."

Once we were married, we had enough of it being just the two of us pretty quickly. We had three kids over the next four years - welcoming two daughters, Hadley and Cooper, and our little man, Macklin, into the world.

I've heard it said that life is a collection of moments, and as for me, I find myself being a moment collector. It's what I've done for the majority of my adult life. It's what I continue to do today. I collect moments. Some of them I've shared very openly. Some of them I've kept to myself.

Millions of moments would come and go throughout the ten years I got to be Rachel's husband. Some of those moments were really beautiful ones. So many beautiful ones. Some of them were really hard, life-altering ones. Some seemed mundane and unimportant at the time, only to become much more significant than we could have ever imagined. Some seemed so enormous that we'd spend hours and even days obsessing over them until they ultimately turned out to be no big deal.

But so many of them have taught me wonderful lessons that have made me the person I am today - a better daddy, a better son, a better friend, a better business partner, a better steward, a better dreamer, a better neighbor, and ultimately just a much better person.

And to think, if it weren't for a silly flag football game in Lincoln, Nebraska, in the middle of winter, none of this would have ever happened. These moments would have never existed. Sure, I'd have made different moments. But these are my favorite moments. Through the ups and downs and highs and lows and all the moments in between, it was the moment when I decided to chase a girl named Rachel that led to the moment she finally caved and said, "I do." That led to my favorite story.

The story of us.

THE RISE

I have a confession to make: I'm unemployable. I've been an entrepreneur all my adult life. I loathe the idea of working for someone else and actually having a real job. Don't get me wrong; I can go get a job (I think). But I don't want to get a job. It's just not in me.

I remember having a conversation with my daughter Hadley when she was about six years old. She told me she wanted to be an entrepreneur – "Just like you, Daddy!"

I asked her why, and she said, "Because you get to pick us up from school and play with us at the park and eat lunch with us every day."

Hadley is her mommy. She looks like her mommy. She thinks like her mommy. She loves like her mommy. She's so smart. She's so kind. She cares deeply for people. And taking care of others is so important to her. I'm telling you, Hadley is her mommy and I'm not sure there is a better compliment that I could ever give someone.

Needless to say, I was so happy to hear that her idea of being an entrepreneur meant being available. It meant showing up. It meant being present. And at the same time, I was relieved to learn that maybe she had forgotten the other side of her daddy being an entrepreneur - the many days when I was so far from any of those things.

Once I got out of college, I knew that I wanted to make it to "the top." Whatever that meant. I just knew I wanted to be there. And I knew getting to the top would take a lot of work, a lot of time, and a lot of hustle. Just a lot. I was the one who woke up the earliest and went to bed the latest. The one whose phone would die the most throughout the day. Not because I was playing games or scrolling social media, but because I was hustling. I was working. I was doing all I could to climb that ladder. I was the one who truly believed that a 60-hour work week was part-time. And I was the one who would take the family to dinner, immediately hop on a phone call as we were being seated, only to come back an hour later to some fussy kids, an annoyed wife, and a boxed meal to go.

If those were the actions of which successful entrepreneurs were built, I for sure made it to the top. I was making good money. I was making a name for myself. I was doing really well. I thought I was "the man." And I think even some others thought I was the man as well. The problem was that I was the man to all the people who really didn't matter that much. And though it looked like I had it all together from the outside looking in, I was on the fast track to failure. A failed marriage. Failed relationships. Failed health. Complete and utter failure.

BUT… I do love entrepreneurship. It's all I know, and as far as I can tell, I still don't have a real job. The good news is that through all of my failures, I learned something really special. You ready for this? You don't have to work 80-hour weeks to win. You don't have to skip dinner each night or be on the phone 24/7 to succeed. You don't have to miss your kids' sporting events or dance recitals to climb to the top. You don't have to neglect the people you love, only to blame it on being the provider.

Instead, do this:

> *"Don't try to change the world. Find something that you love and do it every day. Do that for the rest of your life, and eventually, the world will change."[1]*

I can't claim that as my own. That comes from my boy Macklemore in his song, "Growing Up." If you haven't heard it, you have permission to put the book down and go listen right away. But please come back.

Ok, I just listened to it again. Those lyrics. Just wow.

"Don't want to be a dad that's living in FaceTime, but I got a world to sing to and you at the same time."[1]

Gosh, I could totally keep going. Absolutely craving a jam session right now.

I digress.

I wish they would have taught us this stuff in school. I don't remember a "Pursue your Passion 101" or an "AP - Follow Your Dreams" class. What I do remember is a lot of wasted time and money being taught things that meant very little to me. Yes, school is important. No, do not drop out. Yes, I make my kids go to school. But at the same time, I encourage them to find the things they love and do more of that. And if it's not math, don't do math.

So, find the things that you love. Things you're passionate about. Things that can help others. Things that allow you to do what matters most to you. Like picking your kids up from school and playing at the park. Something that was so obvious to even a six-year-old little girl. Find that something that allows you to do more of the things you love. Do that every single day, and you are now an entrepreneur. An entrepreneur that I look up to and an entrepreneur that I'd love for Hadley to become.

I think it's safe to say that many men long to be providers. It's how many of us are wired. It's super important to us. And for some, it's how we feel adequate. And for others, it's how we show love to our people. Being a provider is a huge deal. And it matters. But I found out the hard way that it didn't matter to my people the way I thought it did.

I remember being taught that if I would just do 10x the work, I'd be 10x more successful. That I'd have 10x the income. That I'd be 10x more well known. And though those things may be true, they never warned me that if work became my idol and if it became all I ever did, I'd likely end up 10x lonelier, 10x

[1]*Songwriters: Ben Haggerty / Ed Sheeran / Joshua Karp / Joshua Rawlings / Owuor Arunga / Ryan Lewis / Tyler Williams Lyrics © Kobalt Music Publishing Ltd., Sony/ATV Music Publishing LLC*

emptier, and 10x more broken. Yes, I'd be driving a fancy car. Yes, I'd own the big, beautiful home. Maybe even a couple of big, beautiful homes. But day after day, if I continued down this path, each night would end by walking into a big beautiful home that was altogether empty.

During my "rise," I had become a master at missing moments, and that's not something I'm proud to say. Honestly, since Rachel and I had gotten married, I'd become a "moment misser." But it escalated to a brand new level soon after our second daughter, Cooper, was born.

Coop is my beautiful mess and brings so much joy into my life. She brings so much joy into the lives of anyone that gets to know her. She hasn't discovered a song that she can't dance to, and she hasn't come across a single person in her entire life that doesn't become a friend. Everyone needs more Cooper in their lives. You may not know it, but it's true.

Around the time she was born, I had just started another business, business number three at the time. I was beginning to make some good money; I was building something pretty impressive. I was making a name for myself in the industry. I was doing big things. I wasn't sleeping much. My phone was dying a bunch of times a day. And if that's happening, you must be working hard. I just kept getting busier and busier. And more and more well known. And I loved it. It was so rewarding. It was so fulfilling. It was awesome. At least, that's what I thought at the time.

I had become a road warrior and had put over 70,000 miles on my car in less than two years. On top of that, you should have seen the Delta SkyMiles® perks I'd unlocked. I was on the go, and I was on a mission. I could be found in house after house, at event after event, closing deal after deal. I was building a massive business. I was becoming a big deal. I was climbing the ladder to success. I was doing it really quickly. And it was awesome. It felt amazing knowing that this rise was going to have such a positive impact on our family. It was going to set us up for life. We would have no worries anymore.

But come to find out, no matter how far up the ladder I climbed, no matter how much money I brought home, no matter how many thousands of people I spoke in front of, the brutal truth resided in the fact that though I'd become "the man" on the road, I'd become the exact opposite in my own home. Because home was the only place I could never be found.

THE RUN

It was late August 2014. There was a rank in my company that I was running after. With that rank would come a bunch of money, a bunch of recognition, and a bunch of praise from a bunch of people. At this point, I'd been on the road for a month straight. Rachel said it was more like four months, but I seem to remember stopping by a few times to do laundry and pretending to be a good husband and a good dad. I was for sure a poser. From the outside looking in, I had it all together. I'd even speak about my happy, perfect little family back home each time I'd hit the stage. And if they'd happen to be at an event, I'd bring them up on the stage with me to show them off. I had mastered the way I would present myself in front of others and on social media, of course. Because to me, at that point in my life, that stuff mattered most.

Looking back, it hurts. It's so sad how awful I was. I cared much more about what thousands of strangers thought about me than what my wife and kids thought about me. I spent much more time trying to impress people from the stage than I did holding space with those that mattered most. And I just kept using the same excuse. I kept telling myself the same story. I was on a mission. I was providing for my family. And that's what mattered. I was going to make it to the top no matter what got in the way. There was no stopping me.

I remember the moment like it was yesterday. I finally hit the rank. The place I'd been working so hard for. I remember celebrating with my team, the CEO, and all the other leaders. Calls were coming in from everyone, from everywhere. I had finally made it into the inner circle, and I couldn't have been happier. It was one of the most significant achievements of my professional career.

Interestingly, the culmination of my rise to grandeur didn't take us anywhere fancy. Instead, it landed us at a Starbucks in Knoxville. Rachel came to meet me so we could celebrate with a few friends. She walked in and collapsed into my arms.

One thing I neglected to mention is that during this run, and over the final weeks of it, we decided to move into a new home. And you already know that there was zero chance I would be able to stop what I was doing to go help with that process. So I left it to Rachel. In the middle of the summer. Oh, and she happened to be six months pregnant with our 3rd child. Oh, and on top of all that, she would need to keep tabs on Hadley and Cooper, who were both in diapers. I mean, can you even fathom there being a bigger jerk on the planet than me?

I didn't think so. Me neither.

"We did it, baby! We made it!" I said as I hugged Rachel as tight as I possibly could.

She fought back what I thought were happy tears, put on her best fake smile, and said, "I'm so happy for you, baby. I really am. It's amazing what you've accomplished. But is there any chance you could please just come home now?"

This was supposed to be a celebration. With our friends. With our team. We had just hit the pinnacle. And somehow, during the entire run, I had missed the fact that all she longed for was for me to come home. She was happy for me. She really was. But she just missed her husband. And she just wanted him to come home.

I'd made it. I'd finally made it. But what this coffee-shop moment caused me to realize is that there is nothing impressive about a man that can lead a massive organization yet fail to lead his family. Some of y'all are in the midst of this right now. Some of y'all are no doubt "the man" at the office, in the boardroom, or from the stage, but at home, you're far from it. I'm allowed to call you out because I was the epitome of this man. And I just want you to realize it before it's too late.

A lot has changed since that run. I still work my butt off. I still hustle. I still strive for success. Heck, I just started another business earlier this year. I still do whatever it takes to provide for my family. But my definition of being a provider and what success looks like has changed a ton. Today, success looks like getting my work done by 2:52 p.m. each afternoon so I can meet the kids at the bus stop. It looks like having dinner with them each and every night. An uninterrupted, no phones allowed dinner. It looks like never allowing my kids to think a phone call or an email matters more than they do. Yes, I still work hard. But no, I don't idolize it like I once did. This was far from a simple overnight fix. This took a whole lot of work. And a moment you won't even believe.

THE MOMENT

After that super awkward "come home" moment with Rachel at Starbucks, I went home. For about a week. But things weren't slowing down. She knew it, and I knew it. We were a couple of months away from welcoming another little one into the world. I told Rachel it would get better. I told her that I'd find a balance. That I had it under control. I told her to just trust me. And she said she did. I'm not sure why she did. But she did.

Things were crazy. Remember, I'd mastered what I looked like to the outside world. And according to them, I had it all together. I was a family man, a great business mind, an excellent team builder, a fantastic speaker, etc. And people wanted my time. They were willing to pay a lot of money for my time. People began hiring me to speak to their teams, their companies, and their students. To be honest, I really couldn't believe this was all happening.

I loved every moment of it. I loved being on stage. I loved empowering other teams and organizations. I had found my calling. I thought I was really good at it and never got tired of hearing others tell me how good I was at it. I really couldn't believe that people would pay me to show up and talk about things that I loved talking about. And as long as they were willing to ask me to show up, I was going to show up.

Around this time, when it came to my home life, I thought I had made strides in the right direction. I believed that I was doing better. I was home a little bit more. I'd usually spend a week away and then a week at home. This was me making up for lost time. I thought this was a great compromise. My little man had arrived, and it was nice to have another man in the house. I knew he'd be watching me and hoped he'd want to be just like me. And I liked the person I was and thought if he grew up to be like me, that would be pretty cool.

I remember one night shortly after Macklin was born, I was getting Hadley ready for bed. She had this super cute thing that she would say each night (when I was actually around) as I'd place the covers over her and kiss her goodnight.

"Daddy, please stay." Meaning, "Please don't leave until I fall asleep."

And I'd always reply, "Of course, Sweetie."

And if I tried to walk out and she hadn't fallen asleep quite yet, she'd just whisper again, "Daddy, please stay."

I'd reply again, "Of course, Sweetie," and I would hold her little hand with one hand and my phone with the other. I'd be checking emails, replying to messages, and scheduling calls, all while getting her to fall asleep. Pretty impressive, huh? Multitasking at its finest.

On this particular night, she said something that I'll never forget and that I still don't think I've forgiven myself for. Literally one of the most eye-opening and crushing moments of my life. I was in the middle of responding to an email when she quietly asked,

"Daddy, do you love your phone more than you love me?"

I can't even write that without tearing up. I'm not sure I ever told Rachel this conversation happened. I'm afraid of what her response would have been. It was the most embarrassing, humbling, and heart-wrenching moment of my life. My four-year-old daughter questioned whether I loved my phone more than her. To her, it only made sense because I spent more time on my phone than I did with her. I missed dinners because of my phone. I missed bathtime and bedtime because of my phone. I missed playtime because of my phone. I missed thousands of little moments because of my phone. To her, it was simple;

time with her was much less important to me than time with my phone.

I knew at that moment something had to change. And by something, I'm referring to me. I was the problem. I had to be better. I had to get it right before Hadley, Cooper, or Macklin grew up believing that I loved anything more than them.

I changed that night. There is no doubt that a major shift occurred. I wasn't perfect. I'm still far from perfect. But I made some significant changes. One practice I put into place right then and there was that when my kids ask me a question or need something or want to hang out, I never answer "soon" or "in a minute." To a kid, what does that even mean? Heck, to an adult, what does that mean? It means "I'm too busy" or "Something else is more important." And that's never something I want my kids to feel. So if I absolutely can't hang with them, I set a time, right at that moment, when I can hang out. I have a long way to go to get this right, but I have stopped saying "soon" because "soon" isn't a time.

I don't know if my heart will ever be fully repaired from that conversation with Hadley. I'm sure she doesn't even remember it, but I will never forget it. Gosh, I hope she doesn't remember it. I hope she wouldn't say that today. I don't think she would, but as I said, I still have a long way to go.

There is a silver lining here. Not too long after that bedtime chat with Hadley, I read something that Lysa TerKeurst wrote about moms that I thought applied to dads as well:

"Bad moments don't make bad moms. God's grace is here to cover us. Teach us. And even in the middle of bad moments, interrupt us, redirect us and change us."[2]

So as bad as I was at that moment, bad moments happen. But bad moments don't make bad dads or bad moms or bad husbands or bad wives or bad friends. That moment with Hadley was the redirect moment that my life needed. That bad moment with Hadley changed my life in an incredible way.

[2] *© 2018 Lysa TerKeurst. Proverbs 31 Ministries.*

It opened my eyes to the reality that we don't get moments back. Once they are gone, they are gone. It reminded me that each day that goes by is a day we won't ever have again. Tomorrow our kids will be a little bit older than they are today. Today is a gift. This moment is a gift. We gotta do better. We gotta show up for one another. We need to notice the little things. To be grateful for all of the things. Because this day, this moment, should be cherished. Because we don't get do-overs.

THE TALK

"But this is my calling, baby!" I explained to Rachel after she told me yet again that I couldn't keep going like this. I was rarely home, and when I was home, I was never truly there. But the way I looked at it, I was doing so much good in the world. I was helping so many people. I was inspiring, uplifting, encouraging, and doing all the other fancy 'ing' words for so many other people.

To which Rachel responded, "I realize you're filling up their tanks, and I so appreciate you for that. But you're leaving my tank empty. I'm tired of chasing you. I'm tired of pursuing you. That's not what I signed up for. I need 'us' to be your calling. I need you to be as excited to lift me up and to encourage me as you are about doing that for complete strangers."

And though, at the time, it felt like a slap in the face, she was so right. It wasn't fair. This wasn't what she signed up for. In our vows, I didn't mention that I'd be on the road for 90% of our lives. I didn't let her know that being married to me would leave her feeling neglected and empty. I didn't prepare her for a life where everyone else would get the good stuff, and she'd be stuck with the leftovers. This wasn't what she signed up for, and it wasn't ok anymore.

It was a Tuesday evening. I was in St. Louis for a work trip and had just returned to my hotel room for the night. I called Rachel and the kids to say goodnight. And as Rachel and I were wrapping up our conversation, the same conversation we had each night, you know the one:

Me: How was your day?
Her: Good.

Me: Good.
Me: How are the kids?
Her: Good.
Me: Good.
Her: How was your meeting?
Me: Good.
Her: That's all?
Me: It was good. I'm just really tired.
Her: Yes, me too.
Me: Ok, well, I'll call you tomorrow. Sleep tight.
Her: Ok. Goodnight. Love you.
Me: Love you too.

And as I was about to hang up, she said, "Wait, what if we just came with you?"

"Excuse me?," I replied.

"Brandon, I can tell you're not going to slow down. You've been saying you would for four years, and it's not getting better. It may even be getting worse. I'm tired. I need my husband. The kids need their daddy. So, what if we just came with you?," she asked.

"You mean, like, everywhere?," I questioned.

"I mean like, yes, everywhere," she replied.

I remember thinking:

Is she crazy? We have a five-year-old, a four-year-old, and a two-year-old. She must be crazy. I didn't want to tell her she's crazy. But this idea was crazy. I can't just bring them everywhere I go. That's not how this works. This is stupid. She will get over this. Maybe she's been drinking. She'll forget about this tomorrow. At least I hope she will.

"Ok, baby, I'm not really sure how this looks, but can we talk about it when I get home?" I asked with hopes that we wouldn't ever talk about this again.

Well, sure enough, 48 hours later, I got home, and it was the first thing we talked about. Turns out she hadn't been drinking that night. Unfortunately. So we talked. And we talked and talked and talked. And you won't even believe what her conclusion was:

"Let's put our stuff into storage, get a motorhome, and go out as a family wherever you need to go for the next year before Hadley starts kindergarten."

I mean, guys, this is crazy, right? Like this is insane, reality TV type crazy, correct? No one in their right mind would choose to do this. We had a great home with plenty of room. Enough room for me to hide for my calls or for work or just to hide out in general. And she's over here saying:

"Let's pack everything up.
Put it in storage.
Leave the comfort of this big ol' house behind.
Find a motorhome. (Meaning a home with wheels on it.)
Buy it.
Put some things in it.
Pack the kids up.
And then just hit the road together?"

There were *so* many problems with this suggestion. To name a few:

1. I don't camp, nor had I ever in my life camped up to this point. We aren't a camping family. I didn't grow up in a camping family. My dad and mom didn't camp. We like hotels and fresh water and showers and comfortable beds. Oh, and plumbing. We want indoor plumbing that doesn't require us to clean up our own feces.

2. I don't drive big rigs. I don't know how. I don't want to learn how. I like my small car and my small SUV.

3. Never in my life had I heard of a family of five doing such a ridiculous thing, and I sure wasn't trying to be the dad to start this trend.

4. I felt like there was a really good possibility that child protective services would come and take our kids from us for putting them in a motorhome with no plan. No driver. No idea where we were going. It just seemed like the kids would be in an unsafe and unfit environment.

5. People would think we were crazy. I didn't want to invite people into our lives that would talk about how crazy we were. Maybe it was pride. Ok, fine, it was for sure pride. But call me prideful; I didn't want people to talk stuff about us.

Fast forward to three weeks later. In July of 2016, Rachel and I boarded a plane for Florida to pick up a 40-foot motorhome that our family would call home for the next 365 days.

THE AHA

Before we jump into our time in the RV, I have something important to say. An "aha" really. As you can see, the RV was all Rachel's idea. And once she set her mind on it happening, there was no turning back. This really mattered to her. And what's important to understand here is that a wife who feels loved and heard is an unstoppable force. A wife who knows that she is seen and noticed can dream big. She can persevere. She can flourish. She can take risks and jump. And she knows that it's ok to fall. Because it doesn't matter what's in front of her as long as she knows who is there to catch her.

There were way too many times in our marriage when I knew Rachel didn't feel like I was there to catch her. I think there were probably many times she wanted to jump, but she most certainly knew what the result would be. I was too busy with work. I had too many projects going on. I was too selfish. I was too focused on my problems to take the time to notice hers. I can't imagine being in her shoes. I'm so thankful for her patience with me. I'm thankful she continued to stay by my side. And I'm thankful that no matter what, she was always there to catch me when I fell. And believe me, I fell a lot.

But mostly, I'm thankful that she always let me be a hero in the eyes of my kids. No matter how absent I was, Rachel still allowed me to hang the moon in their eyes. I was still perfect to them. They still ran into my arms each time I walked into a room. They still wanted daddy time no matter how much I neglected them. And the only reason for this is because Rachel allowed them to adore me. She had every reason to bash me when I was gone. The kids had many opportunities to overhear

Rachel talking badly about me with her friends. But they didn't hear it because it didn't happen. She allowed me to continue to be my kids' superhero no matter how bad I got. No matter how absent I was. And because of that and many other things, Rachel is the superhero that I never deserved.

I'm so thankful to have people in my life that will call me out. That will stand up to me if they see that I'm out of line or that my priorities are off. If you don't have these people, I encourage you to invite them in and give them permission to be that for you. For me, most often this person was Rachel, but sometimes it was and continues to be my parents. Sometimes it was and continues to be my brother, my sister-in-law, or my sister. Other times it's been friends. Friends that know the not-so-pretty side of me and that I've allowed to call me out when I suck. This is so important. We don't always have to figure this stuff out on our own. All too often, we can't see our own faults. Invite people in. You'll be better for it.

THE RV

40 FEET OF...FUN??

And the adventure begins. Oh, the stories we could tell. Some of them I'll let y'all in on; some should probably be left untold. And we should have known that the upcoming year was going to look a bit different given what the first 24 hours threw our way.

In route to retrieve our home on wheels, we had two canceled flights, a rental car experience that could have only taken place in a Seinfeld episode, and an 85-year-old man that gave me one piece of driving advice on what it took to be behind the wheel of a 40-foot RV:

"It doesn't really matter what you do. You're bigger than all the other cars on the road; they will get out of your way."

That was it. That's all I got. That was my driving lesson.

Other than the fact that the first time I was behind the wheel, I went the wrong way on a one-way road...and that just a couple of hours later, all the lights and controls in the rig shut off... and the fact that we spent our first night in our new home in the middle of Nowhere, Georgia...in a pitch black RV...in a Wal-Mart parking lot, everything was perfect. Oh, the nights we spent in Wal-Mart parking lots. Oh, the stories we could tell.

What should have been about a seven-hour drive from Tallahassee to Knoxville, turned into closer to 24 hours. The plan was to get the rig to Knoxville, pack the kids up, grab a few necessities, and then hit the road. That was our plan. Oh, the plans that this RV would ruin.

Instead of going to get the kids upon our arrival in Knoxville, we headed straight to a local RV service center to get the lights fixed and make sure this thing was road-worthy before we took off for good. We thought it was going to be a quick fix. They told us it would be a day or two. We thought it would just be a couple of fuses and maybe a wire here and there. We thought. And man, did we think wrong.

Remember, this was our home. We didn't have another place to live. Someone else was already living in our house, which technically wasn't even ours anymore. All of our stuff was packed up in storage. We didn't have a backup plan. And little did we know at the time, we wouldn't get our RV back...I mean, we wouldn't get our home back...for an entire month. Yep, that's right. We were now homeless. What was supposed to be this super fun, super exciting adventure began with us teaching the kids what it's like to not have a home.

Now don't feel too bad for us. We weren't living on the streets. I didn't send the kids to different intersections with signs begging for money. I mean, looking back, that probably would have been a great idea. I bet we could have done pretty well. Rachel and three toddlers with a cardboard sign saying, "Homeless and hungry." It wouldn't have been a lie. The kids were always hungry, and we were absolutely homeless. But I thought a little more about it and didn't love the idea of my family panhandling. The truth is that we were lucky to have family and friends around who were always willing to open their doors and welcome us into their homes. We never missed a meal. We always had a place to sleep. And though we didn't have a place to call home, and though it was super frustrating, we were all together...and that was the whole reason we were doing what we were doing.

I learned pretty quickly that patience was going to be the key to surviving this year. Nobody in the RV world was in a hurry. Heck, most were retired and had nowhere to be. But we did. We weren't them. I had work to do and places to go. But the RV shop didn't seem to care and never really paid any attention to my sob story. I called them every single day that month, looking for an update. Most days, I would also stop by, and it was always the same thing – "Waiting on a part, should be ready in the next few days." Every day. For an entire month.

Long story short, there were more than just a couple of fuses and a wire or two that needed to be fixed. There were a ton of issues with the rig. It turns out that while it was in storage down in Florida, a family of rats had decided to move in and feast on the wires. I was told that anything that could corrode had corroded and needed to be replaced. It was wild because from the outside looking in, this thing was awesome. The outside looked incredible, but the inside was a complete mess. The stuff you couldn't see wasn't any good. There is probably a life lesson hidden in there somewhere. Beautiful from the outside but can't even function because of what was going on inside.

I'm not sure I can remember what the final bill was for that month-long stay in the repair shop. I'm pretty sure I chose to block that out of my memory. But I do remember the number being so big that when I saw it, at that exact moment, I knew that Hadley, Cooper, and Macklin may not be able to attend college like we'd planned. It was gross. It was really gross. But there was nothing we could do about it, and we were just thrilled to have our home back. The adventure could finally begin. Well, at least that was the plan.

Rachel and I had a mini vacation planned right as we were about to get our home on wheels back. And while we were gone, we had to get the RV from Knoxville to St. Louis for an event we needed to attend. We just happened to have some very dear friends that were willing to make that happen for us. They were RV experts, and we felt so comfortable with them behind the wheel. We also knew they would be able to help us learn a little more about what was working, what was not, and what we'd need to make this year more comfortable.

Other than the fact that the refrigerator wouldn't get cold and that one of the outside storage doors popped open and snapped off while going 70 mph, nearly causing a fatal accident, their trip was pretty uneventful. I was just thrilled that I wasn't heading to St. Louis facing manslaughter charges. In the end, the refrigerator was an easy fix, and the storage door only cost us about $700 and a few more days of homelessness. Maybe now was the time we could finally begin our adventure…perhaps.

The thing is, I could literally write an entire book, maybe even two books, on the mishaps, hiccups, headaches, and struggles that came with RV living. Believe me when I tell you that there were many nights spent in places kids should never spend nights. There were many moments when I wanted to throw in the towel. There were a few too many 3:00 a.m. breakdowns that left me in tears, wondering what the heck I'd gotten my family into. There were so many hard moments. Moments that should have broken us. But when all was said and done, I wouldn't have traded any of the moments, no matter how bad things got, for the lessons that we learned from the road that year.

As you read on, I'm going to talk about some of those lessons. I'm going to dive into some of the really great moments and at the same time jump into some of the hard ones. And what you'll learn pretty quickly is that these weren't lessons that I was teaching. I was the student here. These were lessons that my kids taught me. These were lessons that Rachel taught me. And these were lessons complete strangers, who I would otherwise never come in contact with, taught me.

The adventure was finally on, and we were heading into a season that would change our lives in ways we'd never imagined.

All because one day, Rachel decided that enough was enough and made it clear that from now on, "We are coming with you."

LESSON 1:
"WHO IS YOUR NAME?"

People are so good. I mean, I knew people were good, but during our year on the road, I learned that most people are so dang good. One of the interesting things about the RV life is that, more often than not, the majority of the people that we came in contact with were quite different from us. Their way of life was not what we were typically used to. Normally, we are drawn to people just like us. I'm sure you're the same. People that have the same interests. Root for the same teams. Go to the same church. Vote for the same people. Live in the same neighborhood. Have similar beliefs. Dress the same. Act the same. Even look the same. Those are the type of people that become our people. And it's really easy because they are just like us. And we like us. A lot.

The "RV people" weren't like us. They were so much different than us. We learned pretty quickly that everyone chooses the RV life for a different reason. All under different circumstances. Some were super rich, and their million-dollar motorhomes showed that quite clearly. Some didn't have a dime to their name, and you wondered how their motorhome was even habitable. Some were super young and just getting started with their lives. Some were super old and planned to travel until they could travel no more.

But man, these people were so good. They would lend a helping hand, looking for nothing in return. They would keep an eye out for you, for your stuff, for your kids, and they just had a way of making you feel safe. They would make you feel at home, knowing full well that you didn't even have a home. They didn't care who you voted for or what your motorhome looked like. They didn't care where you went to church or whether you went to church at all. They didn't care what neighborhood you were from or what you believed. It didn't matter to them if you were going to be there for a few days, a few weeks, or a few months. They just showed up. They just cared for people. These people loved people. These people quickly became our people. And I want to introduce you to one of my favorites of all these people.

It was the middle of winter, and we needed to spend some time in Columbia, Missouri. It wasn't that mid-Missouri in the middle of the winter sounded like a great place to be. I just happened to have some business there, and it was just where we were called to be during that season. Many wise people told us to "go south for the winter," and though we didn't listen to them, those people were so right. Because we chose this climate to spend our winter months in, most mornings we would wake up to frozen pipes which, of course, meant no water. Which meant no showers. Which meant no coffee. Don't even get me started on how it makes me feel to start my day with no shower and no coffee. But we did it. Somehow we did it. I still don't know how. But I'm here today to tell you that we did it.

There was a peculiar man that happened to be staying at the same park that we were that winter. And if I'm being completely honest, I just wasn't comfortable with him. Something was off, and he just rubbed me the wrong way. He was really old. But for what it's worth, I love old people, so that wasn't the issue. I'm just trying to paint a picture here. He was messy. Actually, sloppy might be a better word. Yep, he was sloppy, and I'm certain that he hadn't shaved or had a haircut in decades. And there isn't a chance in the world that he'd showered that month. He was really quiet and kept to himself. He was alone. Well, he had a couple of little dogs, but other than that, he was alone. He stayed out of everyone's way and never got into anyone's business. He didn't have a fancy motorhome like we did. From the looks of him and his campsite, he didn't have much at all. He had an old beat-up trailer and an even older beat-up pickup truck. I just assumed he was running from something and found a place to hide, which happened to be a little too close to us for my comfort.

We didn't have to cross his path much, seeing that his trailer was parked at the very opposite end of the park from ours. I was happy about that. Because this man wasn't like us. We were way too different. And as far as I was concerned, it was best to just keep our distance.

Wait, I've got it! Do you remember Kevin McAllister's neighbor in *Home Alone*? He reminded me of that guy. Old Man Marley. That was this guy. He was, for sure, Old Man Marley. And no one in their right mind would approach Old Man Marley. Not you, not me, not our children, nobody.

He reminded me of that person that is in the aisle that you're trying to go down at the grocery store, but you stall for a little while until they leave because you don't want to get too close. Don't act like I'm the only one. We've all been there. Don't pretend like you haven't been there. You've for sure been there.

My plan was to never have a conversation with this guy. I was content to avoid him the entire time we were there. He was way too different from me. There was no way we had anything in common. I hate to admit this, but I would have never said a word to him had it not been for Cooper asking him one little question one afternoon. A question that would forever change the way I view people. Yep, it took a 4-year-old little girl asking a simple question to the scariest man I'd ever seen.

Missouri in the winter is a strange place. It can be 10 degrees with blizzard-like conditions one moment, and then like 12 minutes later, it's 55 and sunny. It was one of those sunny afternoons when we found ourselves where we'd often find ourselves whenever the weather allowed it, the RV park playground. Old Man Marley was out walking his dogs and was coming down the path that would eventually cause him to walk uncomfortably close to us. It was the only path there was, so it wasn't like there was any other way for him to go. But still, at that moment, I wished he'd have found another route. Now, when I say he was uncomfortably close, that may be a slight exaggeration. The path was probably 30 or 40 feet from the bench I was sitting on. But still, that was just a little too close. Remember who we were dealing with, people. The guy with the shovel in *Home Alone*! He was close enough to the playground to be noticed but not close enough where I had to take notice. I just did what I do best and ignored him.

But not Cooper. Once she saw him getting close, she flew down the slide as fast as she could and darted toward me. I assumed she was running to me so I could protect her. I assumed wrong. I sat in shock as she ran by me and stood right at the edge of the playground, where it met the walking path that the axe murderer was walking on. She stared him up and down.

I sat frozen. Macklin and Hadley froze as well. We all went numb. This had all the makings of a future Dateline episode. Probably titled something like "Marley, The Motorhome Murderer."

As he got within a few feet of her, I snapped out of my frozen state and began walking over to Coop to protect her, but before I could swoop in and save her life, she simply smiled and said, "Hi, my name is Cooper. Who is your name?"

I think he was a little taken aback. Kids didn't approach and introduce themselves to this man. And you could tell he wasn't expecting this interaction. After his initial shock wore off, he responded kindly, "Hi, sweetie, my name is Mark."

"Nice to meet you, Mr. Mark," replied Cooper as she ran as fast as she could to the tire swing where her brother and sister were waiting with anticipation for her safe return.

Because my 4-year-old daughter decided to be kinder than her dad and ask a complete stranger, "Who is your name?," I got to become friends with one of the most amazing humans I've ever met.

His name is not Old Man Marley. His name is Mr. Mark, and he is so much of what's right with the world. He is so kind. He is so generous. He is so selfless. And it turns out he wasn't at an RV park in Columbia, Missouri, hiding from anyone or running from anything. He was there because his mom lived about a mile away, and she wasn't doing well. He left the comfort of his home in Texas to tow a beat-up RV with a beat-up truck to be close to his mom, who needed his help.

This man was such a good man. It turns out that Mr. Mark fought for our country. Actually, he jumped out of planes, and oh, the stories he could tell. It became one of our favorite nightly traditions, sitting around the campfire, listening to Mr. Mark tell incredible stories from his life. Where he'd been. Who he'd met. What he'd seen. And all of the things in between.

I guess you could say that Mr. Mark became a part of our family over the next few months. Our travels would see us come and go, but we'd always anticipate getting back to Missouri to see Mr. Mark.

People are so dang good. And Mr. Mark is the definition of what so dang good looks like. And to think, I ignored him for as long as I possibly could. After meeting Mr. Mark, and the circumstances which caused it to happen, I often wonder how many incredible people I've missed out on getting to know in my life because they didn't look like me or act like me or talk like me.

After a few long, cold months in Missouri, the time had come to say goodbye and hit the road for good this time. Although we'd said our goodbyes the night before, as we were pulling out of the park passing Mr. Mark's trailer, the kids begged me to stop so they could give him just one more hug. I just couldn't say no to that request. After the kids had given their hugs and said their final goodbyes, as they jumped back into the RV, Mr. Mark grabbed me by the arm and said something I'll never forget.

As tears welled up in his eyes, he said, "Son, thank you for allowing your wife and your kids to love me like they have. That doesn't happen very often for me. You'll never know how much your family has impacted my life." He continued, "You know if you ever need anything, anything at all, I'm just a phone call away, and you know where to find me."

After I thanked him for saying those things and began saying some of the same stuff back to him, he stopped me and said, "Son, you don't need to say anything else. I just need you to know that I like you, but I love Rachel and those damn kids. And I'd take a dang bullet for you, your wife, and those kids anytime, anyplace, anywhere."

And to think, when we arrived, this was a man I feared might put a bullet in me one day. Little did I know, he was a man that was willing to take one for me, my wife, and my kids, anytime, anyplace, anywhere.

Mr. Mark is the good that I almost missed. That I certainly would have missed had it not been for one little question from one little girl. I don't know whether Mr. Mark realizes it or not, but I needed him much more than he ever needed me. Meeting him and getting to know him made me want to be a better person. Because of how he showed up and loved us, he taught me what it looks like to truly love your neighbor. Sometimes I forget that when Jesus gave us that "Love your Neighbor" command, He knew our neighbor would act, look, talk, believe, vote, and even love differently than us. And I think that was kind of His whole point.

JUST DO! CHALLENGE:

Maybe it's just me, but do me a favor and really think about this. Do you have any people in your life that you do your best to avoid? Some you may know, some you may not. Maybe it's a co-worker? A classmate? Someone from your church? The barista at your local Starbucks? The homeless guy on the corner? Do you ever stop and wonder what their story could be? Do you ever wonder what would happen if we stopped avoiding the avoidable and started showing up for them? Do you ever wonder what would happen if we asked these people one simple question? Four little words. I dare you to do it. I dare you to ask them, "Who is your name?"

LESSON 2:
"THESE ARE THE BEST DAYS!"

I'll often catch myself looking back at our RV year and wish we could rewind back to that time. I'd give anything to be able to do it all over again. I'm so glad we did it, but I just long for more of it. That year went by so quickly, and there was just so much more we wanted to do. But at the same time, I am so grateful for all the little memories we made along the road that year. We made it to Canada but never made it to California. We made it to the Smoky Mountains but never quite got to the Rocky Mountains. We spent some time in Niagara Falls but not even one day in Sioux Falls (not sure Sioux Falls was even on the list, but it just sounded good.)

As our time went by and I became more comfortable behind the wheel of the big rig, I began to really enjoy the long drives we'd often take. The old man was right when he gave me my driving lesson. We were bigger than everyone else, and everyone else just got out of our way. Needless to say, I wasn't afraid of anyone on the road anymore. I may have run a car or two onto the median, but I was never the cause of an actual car wreck. Well, not one that I know of or that I was held responsible for.

One of our longest trips was an excursion from St. Louis to Canada, where Niagara Falls would be our final destination. We'd never been to Canada and couldn't wait to see what was in store for us. We didn't make it a habit of driving late at night, but on the route we were on, we didn't have a ton of other options. It was pretty late, closing in on 11 p.m. I assumed everyone was sleeping because that's what people do at that time of night, but at some point, something must have woken Hadley up. She then proceeded to do something she'd often do on our long road trips. She came up to the front to be my co-pilot. Our little late-night conversations during our drives were some of my favorite times. Yes, she was sitting in the front seat. Yes, she was buckled up. No, you can't judge me. I mean, you can, but don't. Please. Thank you. To be honest, I don't even think it was against the law. I don't remember there being a ton of laws in that thing. I mean, we got up and peed while we drove. We'd make sandwiches, coffee, and other things while we drove. I feel like if I can pee and drive, and that's not against the law, all bets are off.

Anyway, on this particular night, Hadley, who was five years old at the time, said something that happened to be exactly what I needed to hear at that moment. "Daddy, I'm going to miss these days. These are the best days of my life."

I mean, she's five. She's got a whole lot of life ahead of her, and I hope and pray that she comes across some more "best days." And I'm going to do everything in my power to make sure that happens. But for me to hear that, at that moment, it just made me realize that what we were doing was right. I doubted it many times. Each time we would encounter RV trouble, and we'd get stuck in some shady town, at some shady truck stop that served some shady coffee, I'd kick myself for putting us in that situation. Each time the pipes would freeze, or the AC would break, I wondered what the heck we were doing and how I could put my family through this. I know that so many people didn't agree with our plan and doubted Rachel and me for making this decision to hit the road with our kids. For what it's worth, from my perspective, I get it and understand why someone would have felt that way.

But then Hadley said what she said, and at that moment, I realized that all the crappy stuff that came along with the RV life never mattered one bit to Hadley. She will never remember the shady truck stops because, to her, all she saw was that fantastic Icee® machine. She will never remember the frozen pipes because, to her, all that mattered was that she didn't have to take a bath that day. To me, this stuff was all so inconvenient, but to her, it was all so beautiful.

I, too, was going to miss these days. These were my favorite days. These were the best days. The days of camping in the middle of nowhere. The days of fishing every single morning as the sun rose. The days of chasing down the ice cream man, riding scooters for hours, digging holes miles deep, having endless picnics, and enjoying late-night hide-and-seek marathons.

Hadley was so right. These were the days when she got to live in a land of make-believe. Where I got to be the king, and she got to be a princess. These days were so carefree, and these were the days where she got to see the world exactly how she wanted it to be. And I loved the way she saw the world. These were the days when I just wanted so badly to see the world through her eyes. But at the same time, I wished that each of my kids could see themselves through mine. Because I can watch them for a single moment and find a million little things that I love about them.

These were the days when I got the opportunity to closely watch how my kids interacted with all the people that came into their lives. I got to see how they created instant relationships with each and every one of them. I got to witness how much they were loved by everyone who had the chance to meet them. But more importantly, I got to watch the way that they loved others. It didn't matter to them one bit about where they were from, what they did for a living, or what they believed. These were the days when I was supposed to be teaching them life's most valuable lessons, but instead, they were teaching me.

I knew the days of the RV life would eventually come to an end, but that didn't mean these "best days" needed to. These are still the days when I get to continue to prove to my kids how much they matter to me and how treasured they are, not just by buying them things or taking them places, but by showing them with my actions.

These are still the days I get to teach them life's most valuable lessons. Important things like: never pass a lemonade stand, always over-pay, and no matter how bad the lemonade may taste, always say it's perfect.

There are still the days I get to encourage them to ask for extra sprinkles on their ice cream, even if it's an upcharge, because you can never have enough sprinkles.

These are still the days when I move heaven and earth to be present at every ballgame, dance recital, school play, and anything else that's important to them. Oh by the way, it's all important to them.

These are still the days when I do whatever it takes to be there for them and with them, so they know that the little things of today matter just as much as the big things yet to come.

Someday they will have plenty of time to learn about make-up, math, and making out. Someday, probably really soon, they will figure out that I'm not as cool as they think I am. Someday they will even discover for themselves all the beauty and, unfortunately, some of the really hard and not-so-beautiful things that this world has to offer.

I think the hardest dilemma in all of this is that these "best days" in our children's lives can often be the busiest days in our own. The Days when the expectations at work continue to grow. The days when the meetings become a priority over the ballgames or our kids' bedtimes. And every day, it seems that the world will drag us by the arm, trying to convince us that this is more important than that. That the work can't wait. That the number has to get hit. That the calls must be made. That this is the most important thing right now, and that *that* can wait.

The thing that the world doesn't seem to grasp is that our kids aren't going to be kids for long. And that we can't ever get these days back. But I'll let you in on a quick secret: It really is amazing what happened when I told the client that I had to run and that I'd need to get back to them tomorrow. Or when I informed my boss that I had to miss a little bit of the meeting to make sure I didn't miss a minute of my son's ballgame. Are you ready for this? Nothing. Not a thing happened. The client got the call the next day, and the meeting went on just fine. But most importantly, when that first pitch was thrown, and my little man looked up into the stands, he saw me, and his smile said it all. And it was the perfect reminder, "Yes, *this* is what's most important."

Because these days are the best days.

JUST DO! CHALLENGE:

Who do you allow to dictate your days? Does it feel like sometimes you're allowing the world to drag you from one thing to the next? Do you feel like you're missing a lot of moments? Those moments that matter most? What adjustments could you make to miss even just a little less? Maybe you are missing bedtimes,. Try for just one week to make them all. Maybe you are missing ballgames. Try for just one week to make them all. Maybe you are missing dinners with the family. Try for just one week to make them all. We don't get do-overs, and we don't get these moments back. I challenge you today to do your very best to take advantage of the moments that today has to offer.

LESSON 3:
"BECAUSE I WATCH YOU."
(THIS ONE'S FOR THE DADS, BUT MOMS SHOULD READ IT TOO!)

One of the things that Rachel and I learned rather quickly while living in a 40-foot space, other than the fact that there was literally nowhere to go for peace and quiet, was that each of our three kids was so different from their siblings. I mean, we knew that they were each different, but when you have nowhere to go and you can't escape them, it's seen on a whole other level. It became more and more apparent to us that they each had their own needs and their own desires. They liked to do different things, and they had different dreams. And though it's easier to group them up and just do all the days together, it's important to take some time with each of them individually. To allow them to do their own things and chase their own dreams.

One of the practices that Rachel and I put into place during our time in the RV was that at least once a month, we would have individual date days with the kids. Those were days when we would spend some alone time with each of them, separate from the others. Those days became so special to us. Not just for the kids, but for Rachel and me as well. They became some of the most precious times we had that year.

We'd always let them choose what they wanted to do, and the differences between the three were so funny. But especially with the girls. Hadley was, and still is, so simple. More often than not, she'd choose dinner and a movie. Or sometimes a trip to the driving range and a snack in the clubhouse. And ice cream, for sure. There was always ice cream. But it was important to her that it wasn't anything fancy or anything that she'd have to dress up for.

Cooper was, and still is, the exact opposite. She needed to make sure her nails were done. She absolutely wanted enough time to curl her hair, and she didn't do date day in anything less than a dress. Cooper's dates always included shopping. Her favorite spots were Von Marr or Nordstrom. It was important to her that while shopping, someone was playing a piano. Cooper wanted fancy, wanted to be seen, and wanted to dress up.

Then there was Macklin. His date days were filled with guy stuff, even if he was having a day with his mommy. There would be lots of riding scooters, playing with monster trucks, and wrestling. Often, we would catch a ballgame or go watch the airplanes or choo-choo trains. But one of our favorite things to do, when it was just him and me, was to go to the barbershop and "take a haircut." To this day, he still refers to it that way. Never "Get a haircut," always, "Take a haircut." And I love it.

We are dudes, and we needed dude days. I mean, the poor kid rode a pink bike and a pink scooter that his sisters handed down to him. There were many days he would be seen rockin' pink princess headphones while holding his sister's pink iPad. My man had no shame. His sisters would make him play dress-up, and often it would end up with him all made up. He rarely got any say as to what was on the TV because it was always two against one. And he was always outvoted. But Macklin is all boy, and our boys' days were, and still are, so important. Not just for him, but maybe even more for me.

One of my favorite parts of these boys' days was the conversations we would have and all the things I'd learn if I'd simply be present and listen to what Mack had to say. I realize that it was supposed to be the other way around. I know that I was supposed to be teaching him, but the fact is that in many seasons of life, I've learned more from him than I could have ever thought possible.

I always tried to make it a point to have "boy talk" during these moments. We didn't get enough time alone, so I longed to make the most of the moments when we had them.

On one of these days in particular, while we were watching airplanes land and eating ice cream, we started talking about what it means to respect women and how important it is to do so. I explained to him that you should always open the door for your sisters. To make sure you respect your mommy, your mimi, your grandma, and any other girl that you ever meet. To be kind. To protect them and always make sure that they feel safe. In the middle of this conversation with Macklin, he stopped me and said, "Daddy, I know this because I watch you."

My first thought was, *That's right, you do*. And I absolutely do those things all the time, without fail. But then I remembered how I lost my patience with his mommy that morning and overreacted to something so stupid. I thought of the time the week prior when I wasn't so kind to the waitress that kept messing up our order. I didn't yell. I wasn't rude to her face, but the things I said under my breath - but loud enough for Rach and the kids to hear - weren't even close to kind.

"I know this because I watch you."

Man, that slapped me right across the face. I fail way too often. I lose my patience. I get lazy and don't always open doors. I'm not always as kind as I should be. I'm telling him to do one thing, and so often I'm doing the opposite. He's watching. He sees it all. The good and the bad and the ugly. And, like it or not, he is going to grow up to be just like me.

He wants to wear what I wear. He wants to say what I say. He wants to do what I do.

I want to teach him to treat people kindly. All people. Not just some people, but all people. He's watching how I treat people.

I want to teach him that no one loves everyone perfectly except Jesus, but we should strive every day to love people like Jesus does. Mack is watching how I love.

53

I want to encourage him to find what people in his life love to do and go be with them in it, not just in proximity but in presence. He's watching how I interact with those that aren't like me.

I want to show him, not just tell him, that selfless service is the pinnacle of being truly fulfilled. He's watching and learning from me how to serve others.

I want to teach him that the closer he gets to Jesus, the more he will stand out, and that it's ok to stand out. He's watching how I pursue Jesus.

I want to inspire him to give his very best every single day. His best help, his best advice, his best knowledge, his best everything to all those he encounters. He's watching me even on the days when I'm lazy and have very little to give.

I want to teach him to ask people how their day is and then to listen to what they say. Then I want to encourage him to ask them a follow-up question. No one expects a follow-up question. It's amazing what you can learn about people with a simple follow-up question. He's watching the way I communicate with all those I come in contact with.

I want to let him know that God answers our prayers - not according to what we've prayed - but according to what we would've prayed had we known everything He knows. So just to be patient in prayer. He's watching my prayer life.

I want to teach him that it's ok to worry. But not to spend too much time doing so. I want him to understand that today is the tomorrow we worried about yesterday, and the worry of the past never does a thing for the future. He's watching the way I handle stress and the burdens that life brings.

I want him to know that he must always protect his sisters, his momma, his mimi, his grandma, and any other woman that comes into his life. I want him to know that it's not ok to fight, but if someone hurts a woman in his life, he can go full Batman on them. He's watching me and the way I make the women that are most important in his life feel safe.

I pray that I teach him well. I pray that I love him well. I pray that when he's 18 or 58 or 98, he will still want to be just like his Daddy. And I pray that as he watches me, I'll lead him right. I know he may not listen to all the things I say, but I'm certain he will imitate all the things I do. I pray that I practice the things I preach.

As dads, one of our biggest responsibilities in life is understanding that our sons are going to treat their future wives just like they saw us treat their mommies. And our daughters are going to choose to date and eventually even marry a man just like us. A man that treats them like we treat them. A man that cares for them as we care for them. A man that protects them as we protect them. And a man that loves them as we love them.

To be honest, I stumble all the time, but I still pray that my girls compare every man that comes into their lives to me. I'm far from perfect, and I mess up way too often. But I love them so well. I protect them. I encourage them, and I treat them with the respect that they so rightly deserve. So when that day comes, and a man comes along that can treat them like their daddy does, love them as their daddy does, encourage them as their daddy does, and protect them as their daddy does, I'll gladly shake that man's hand and allow him to take theirs.

Dads, I realize that on many days all this can be really scary. Maybe not for you. Maybe you've got it all figured out. But I know it is for me. All too often, I know I can be better. I know I can do more. I know I can love harder. But I also realize I'm a work in progress. And whether you know it or not, you are too. What's important to remember is that even on our worst days and in the midst of our very worst moments, there is grace. God gifted us grace because He knew us well enough to know that we were going to mess up. The beauty lies in the fact that God's grace is so much bigger than my bad days. Than your bad days. Than our bad days. Therefore, we'll never be bad enough for Him to tell us He's had enough.

JUST DO! CHALLENGE:

How does it make you feel knowing that your son will grow up to be just like you? He will dress like you dress. Act like you act. Walk like you walk. Talk like you talk. And love like you love. I hope this makes you feel proud. I hope it makes you feel happy. I hope it makes you feel hopeful. I hope. But if it doesn't cause you to feel that way, what kind of changes can you make today to fix it? Maybe they aren't drastic changes. Maybe they are. But he's watching you. And he wants to be just like you. It's not too late. I promise you that it's not. Because of grace.

LESSON 4:
"SHE WRECKED IT."

Rachel never drove the RV. She never really cared to, and to be completely honest, I never really wanted her to. It was just so dang big and awkward, and she was just so dang tiny and not awkward. It's not that it's super hard to drive. It's just super hard to maneuver. If it wasn't for the old man's advice that we are bigger than everyone else on the road, I'm not sure I'd have had the confidence that I did.

Needless to say, his advice was pretty spot on. Without fail, other vehicles always got out of my way but I can't say that was the case for road signs.

When I mentioned above that Rachel had never driven the RV, that wasn't entirely true. She did. Once. It happened after a long stretch of driving on our way from New York to Knoxville. I had driven for about nine straight hours, and she said she would be willing to drive for a little while as long as it was just highway driving. Looking back, I'm baffled by some of the things we did. Sure, let's have you drive a 20,000-pound motorhome at 70 mph with your entire family in tow for the first time ever. That seems reasonable. Gosh, what were we thinking?!

At the time, it seemed like a good idea because I needed a break. The plan was to let her drive for about an hour before we'd boondock for the night at some Wal-Mart parking lot in the middle of Nowhere, Kentucky. For those that are currently doubting some of my decisions on where to allow my family to sleep some nights, we had a great app that would tell us the best and safest spots to boondock. Rest easy, my friends. They were safe.

For those that have no idea what "boondocking" is, some refer to it as "dry camping" - meaning anytime you camp in your RV without water, sewer, or electrical connections. In our case, this just meant crashing for a night here and there in Wal-Mart parking lots. Yes, it's as glamorous as it sounds.

So, back to the first and the last time that Rachel was behind the wheel.

She had driven for about forty-five minutes and was doing amazing, all things considered.

"Rachel, why don't you pull over at the rest stop ahead, and I'll take over from here," I said, knowing there would be some maneuvering in our near future.

"I think I'm good. I'm doing pretty awesome," Rachel replied as if she'd been driving big rigs for her entire life.

"I'm not sure this is the best idea," I responded.

"Do you not trust me?," she asked.

How was I supposed to answer that? What an unfair question to ask me right now.

Well, "No," I said to myself.

But out loud, I said with total hesitation and a ton of doubt, "Well, of course, I trust you, baby. It's just really hard to drive this thing in tight spaces. But yes, I trust you. Go for it."

Before I go on, I must tell you that this was the longest stretch that we had gone where the RV hadn't seen the repair shop. We were probably a month or so strong. I mean, we were on a roll; we had driven to St. Louis, Chicago, Michigan, Canada, and New York; the RV was really starting to feel like home, and that was becoming a really cool thing for us. I just had to tell y'all that before I tell you this:

Our destination for the night was just a few miles up the road, and Rachel convinced me that she had this. The blinker came on and she took the exit like a champ. There were very few cars on the road, so I felt like she was in good shape at this point. As we approached the parking lot, I reminded her one more time that I could take over if she wasn't comfortable. She assured me that she had it under control, almost in a cocky manner, like she had done this a hundred times.

She pulled into the Wal-Mart lot and headed toward a couple of other parked RVs where we'd set up camp for the night. We were home free. One more quick right turn and then the final straightaway to our landing spot.

Oh, that right turn. The right turn heard all around the Wal-Mart parking lot. The right turn that I will never forget. Rachel took it a little too sharp. I sat in the passenger seat, looking out the side view mirror at what was about to happen. It felt like slow motion. A stop sign that Rachel claimed wasn't there when she began the turn grabbed the side of the RV. It proceeded to jerk the awning completely off the side of the rig. It continued to scrape and rip down the entire passenger side; gashing through the paint, tearing off little pieces of our home, making the sound only heard in the worst horror movies.

I didn't understand how such a small sign could do so much damage to such a big rig. The stop sign won that night. It won big. And as I continued to look in the side mirror - and as the RV finally gave up the fight and made it past the stop sign - I noticed it bounced right back into place like nothing had ever happened.

To say I was mad would be a huge understatement. I was furious. It was the scream-at-your-wife, cuss-like-crazy kind of furious. I'm not a screamer or a curser, but if I had been, it would have been loud and R-rated. But instead, I was deathly silent. Not a word. I think Rachel would have rather I screamed and cursed. But I was quiet. Oh, so quiet. Everyone was. We were all processing what just happened out there. And then, to break the silence was Hadley's little voice hesitantly saying, "I think she wrecked it."

I didn't respond. No one responded. But Hadley was right. She did.

As we slowly pulled to where we would be parking for the night, I dreaded seeing how bad it really was. Not because it wasn't fixable. I knew it would be fixable. It was more because we were finally getting this adventure going, and I just knew this would be another hiccup in our plans. I knew we were looking at more time in the shop and a bunch more money spent.

I was so annoyed. I was so angry. I was so tired of things going wrong. And Rachel could feel it. Come to find out, she had called my sister that night and told her that she felt this was as close as our marriage had ever gotten to ending. I'm pretty confident she knew I wasn't going to leave her or, even worse, murder her. But if looks could have killed, she'd have been a goner.

Eventually, I stepped out of the RV and assessed the damage. I'm not a body shop guy, but I didn't like what I saw. Rachel then stepped out and assessed the damage. Since I still didn't have anything nice to say to her, I said nothing. The kids stepped out and assessed the damage. Not really. They just stepped out because we stepped out. But they, too, knew that it wasn't good.

After a few minutes of awkwardness, Rachel walked back into the RV. Hadley and Macklin followed closely behind her. Cooper stayed with me. She just stood by my side in that dark and lonely Wal-Mart parking lot in the middle of Nowhere, Kentucky. I don't know how long we were out there. I just knew I was kind of numb at that point and that I wasn't ready to go talk to Rachel yet. After some time, Coop broke the silence by saying, "Hey, Daddy, I know you're sad, but it's ok. I can help you fix it."

At that moment, the idea of my four-year-old helping me fix something that there was no way I could ever fix didn't help the situation. And though I didn't immediately understand the importance of what she said, after some time, I realized that she was so right. It was ok. It was such a minor thing that I got majorly mad over. It took me the rest of the night to cool down and get my words together to explain to Rachel that it wasn't her that I was mad at; it was the situation.

The worst part of it all wasn't the RV damage. It was the fact that I let something so fixable and so silly get me so mad at Rachel. And the fact that my kids could see how mad I was. Rachel and I were adults, and though it wasn't ok that I allowed the "She wrecked it" moment to get me so upset, I knew she'd be quick to forgive and understand that I'd overreacted. But the kids were just kids. And though they always gave me so much grace, I hated the fact that they saw me act that way.

One of the reasons I think I beat myself up in moments like this is because I never saw my dad visibly mad at my mom. I know that sounds crazy, but it's true. Not one time growing up did I see him get angry with her to the point that he was visibly mad. I don't have any memory of him losing his patience, overreacting, or being a jerk to my mom. Maybe it's just that my mom is perfect. Or maybe it's that she never wrecked an RV in front of us. But I don't think that's it. I just think he had a much better understanding of what really mattered. And he had a much better perspective on all the things that life threw his way. I don't know exactly what it was, but I know for sure that he would have never let that "She wrecked it" moment turn into what I made it.

PS - Mom, I do think you're perfect. But I'm trying to prove a point here, so thanks in advance for letting me do so.

If I could point to anyone in my life that loves most like Jesus, it would be my dad. Growing up, I wanted to be just like him, and as a grown-up, I still feel exactly the same. Kinda takes you back to that whole thing Mack said earlier: "I know because I watch you."

Mack was only two at the time of the stop sign incident, so he probably doesn't remember it at all. But I hate that any of my kids had to watch me in that moment. It wasn't one of my best moments. It wasn't my favorite moment. It definitely wasn't a moment I'd ever planned to write about in a book one day.

The good news for me is that Rachel was always quick to forgive. And though my apology didn't come until the next morning, she forgave me right away. She felt horrible about it all and quickly agreed to give up her RV driving privileges. I told her that was probably a good idea and that her RV driving experience was short, sweet, and expensive.

The crazy thing is that looking back on it now, I'm so glad it happened. I would have never said this at the time, and it took me a few months to understand this, but that moment taught me a super valuable lesson. That was one of the most beautiful things about RV life. Over and over again, it was in the worst times when the best lessons arose.

From that moment on, I made it a point to not only ask for forgiveness from Rachel when I overreacted or got upset with her, but to also ask for forgiveness from the kids. Not just when I got upset with them, but when I got upset with their mommy and they happened to be around to see it.

The day after the stop sign incident, I took each kid aside and explained to them how sorry I was and how this wasn't mommy's fault. I asked them if they would forgive me for being upset at mommy and told them that sometimes daddy just makes mistakes and that I was so sorry. They were very forgiving and seemed to think it was strange that I was even having this talk with them. Maybe it was more for me than for them. But either way, it was so important.

As they get older and daddy continues to mess up, I hope they appreciate the fact that I notice my failures and that I am quick to ask for forgiveness. I realize that forgiveness doesn't change the past, but it does have a way to enhance the future. There is no doubt that as I look back on the "She wrecked it" moment, I'm so thankful for the lessons learned in that Wal-Mart parking lot in the middle of Nowhere, Kentucky when a stop sign jumped out of nowhere and mutilated our home.

JUST DO! CHALLENGE:

Ok, be honest; when was the last time you overreacted over something? Maybe it was this morning when your drive-thru order was wrong. Maybe it was last night when the kids wouldn't settle down. Maybe it was something your spouse did that just rubbed you the wrong way. Looking back, was your response valid? Did you raise your voice? Did you say some things that you probably shouldn't have said? Were you visibly angry? Were your kids around?

First, I want you to give yourself a break and remind you that we are all human and that these things happen. And while we are being honest, I had a moment yesterday where I completely overreacted and raised my voice at my kids for singing too loud. Yep, I know; I'm the perfect one to give you advice because, as you can see, I'm amazing at this stuff. I've got it all figured out! But my point is: it happens. The question is, what's our reaction to it happening? Instead of sweeping it under the rug, how about if we just admit that we messed up? How about we take the blame, say we're sorry, and ask for forgiveness? Not just with our spouse, but with our kids. It's amazing how forgiving and accepting they'll be if we are just willing to put ourselves out there, admit we suck sometimes, and just say we are sorry.

LESSON 5:
DEPOSITS

One of the most rewarding things about taking that huge step of faith - you know, jumping into a motorhome, and hitting the road for an entire year - was that we knew we'd make such great memories along the way. Much of the time, we had no idea what was around the next bend, but we knew that whatever it was, it would lead to something amazing, or scary, or spectacular, or shocking, or all those words wrapped into one.

As parents, we get to make deposits into the memory banks of our children every single day. We have the opportunity to make those memories really good, or unfortunately, in some cases, really bad. The thing is that no matter what, each and every day, we are filling them up.

From the moment Rachel and I had kids, we agreed that we wanted to fill their banks with adventure, not things. We chose to give them stories to tell, not just stuff to show. Traveling the country with thrcc kids under the age of five was never going to be an easy task, but seeing the joy in their eyes as we experienced new adventures around every turn made each moment more than worth it.

I bet some of you are thinking, "Well, it's easy to make great memories when you're traveling in a big ol' RV and showing your kids super cool stuff all over the country." Well, you're right. But let's take the RV out of the equation for a minute. As parents, we are constantly filling our kids' memories with ideas, beliefs, thoughts, dreams, and all kinds of stuff. Those things don't just go away. They are stored. They are there to stay.

My buddy Blake gave a great talk about this at an event I attended a few years ago. Check this out - we all grew up in different places. Different states, different regions, different countries. We all have different political views and different levels of education. We all attend different churches, and we all have different thoughts and ideas. We all grew up differently. But for some reason, when it comes to this, we are all trained to answer these questions exactly the same way:

When we become school age, it's time to go to _____ .
And at school, it's important that we study _____ .
And if we study hard, we will get good _____ .
And if we get good grades, we will get into a good _____ .
And once we graduate college, we should find a good _____ .
And at that job we must work _____ .
And if we work hard, we will make enough _____ .
And now that we have money, it's time that we start a _____ .
And now that our family is growing, we need to buy a _____ .
And eventually, we will begin to save for _____ .
And then, after many years of this cycle, we'll be retired, and we will finally be _____ .

It doesn't matter how many people you do this exercise with. It doesn't matter where they grew up or what they do for a living. The answers will always be the same. Except for the last one. I've heard a couple of answers for the last one. The answer you'll hear most often is that you'll finally be "happy," but some say that you'll finally be "dead."

Either way, both answers are sad.

Nothing about packing up your kids and all your stuff, uprooting your life, and then moving into an RV is in the playbook you see above. Many of the things that our family has chosen to do in our lives doesn't follow the playbook either. And I can honestly say that we are so much better for it.

Unfortunately, most of us were conditioned that this is how things had to be, and we now teach our kids the same thing. All they know is that they must go to school, study hard, get a job, work for 40 years, eventually retire, and then they can finally be happy.

I often look back to that moment when Hadley told me she'd like to be an entrepreneur, just like me. It makes me happy knowing that I was able to flip the script a bit on her. The ideas of becoming an entrepreneur, following your dreams, and pursuing your passion, don't necessarily fall into the standard operating procedure we are trained to abide by in life. It's different. It's not normal. It's weird. It can be scary. But it's an adventure. And it's awesome.

Again, what it all comes back to is that we have so many opportunities to fill our kids' memory banks with some pretty cool stuff. But we can also just as easily mess those memories up with some pretty ugly stuff.

The good news is that if you don't love the environment you're creating for your kids, it's not too late to fix it. It's never too late. No matter what kinds of things have been stored in your children's heads, there is always room for more. It doesn't matter if your kids are old and grown or if they are newborns and just beginning to understand this thing called life. There is always room in the memory banks to make new ones. To make better ones. And to hopefully delete some of the crappy ones.

Maybe you have older kids and are unsure what that looks like. Guess what? There is still time. Start a new tradition. Do something fun. Plan a vacation. If they are local, bring them coffee once in a while. Don't ask if you can. Just do. If they live farther away, pick up the phone and give them a call or FaceTime them instead of just sending a text. Send them flowers, chocolate, or a gift card. Gift them a wine subscription and then gift yourself one too. And when they show up, talk about them with each other. Send them a card with a ten-dollar bill in it and encourage them to go buy some cotton candy or ice cream or something that they loved when they were little. Just do something. Anything that will leave a smile on their face. And that will create a new memory in that bank of theirs.

If they are young, put down your phone. I know this is hard. But actually, put it down. Not in your pocket, not right beside you. Put it down and walk away from it. And if you can't do this, trust me, their memories will be full of the moments you missed because all they saw was the top of your head. Their banks will be stored with the idea that the phone was more important than them. I've been there. Don't go there. It's not a fun place to be. Instead, go outside and play catch. Play hide-and-seek. Wrestle with them. Fly them around the house. Build a snowman. Shoot hoops. Daydream. Go swimming. Put a note in their lunchbox. Date your daughters and always open the door for them. Read with them. Pray with them. Have dinner with them. If they want to dance, dance with them. If they want to sing, sing with them. If they want to play dress up, then dress up. Bring them a cake pop. Play Uno™ and pick-up sticks with them. Buy them Play-Doh™. And then play Play-Doh™. Be there to pick them up from school. Even if it's just once a week. Maybe it's just on Wednesdays. I promise you, they'll remember the Wednesdays.

Show up. Be present. And fill their banks with the good stuff.

And finally, if you're a dad and you're reading this, turn Saturday into "Dadurday." Or "Momerday" if you're a mom. "Momerday" just doesn't sound as cool. But for real. If you're a dad and you're not having "Dadurday" with your kids, then you're missing out.

I think I was the originator of this. I've seen imitators, and someone even trademarked the word, so whoever you are, you stole my thing. But I'm not mad. Just use it well.

"Dadurday" doesn't have to be extravagant. You don't have to go big here. It can be a donut date in the morning. It can be a movie. It can be a trip to the mall or a round of putt-putt. If money is tight, it doesn't have to cost a thing. It can be a walk, a bike ride, a trip to the park, or a day of fishing. It doesn't matter, but eventually, you'll find that your kids begin to refer to Saturday as "Dadurday." And in that moment, you'll realize that you've made an awesome deposit in their banks. You can't take that away from them. And it's so cool.

I must warn you. Don't commit to "Dadurday" if you're going to screw it up and give it a bad name. You've gotta show up. You've gotta be present. You've gotta own this. It shouldn't be something you have to drag your kids into doing. They should be looking forward to it. If not, you're not doing it right. And it sure shouldn't be something they have to drag you to do. If they do, you're not doing it right. So far my kids are still young enough to love it and to look forward to it each weekend. The cool thing is that I still love "Dadurdays" with my dad, too, so there is hope that maybe my kids won't grow out of it.

As my friend Bob Goff says, "I think a father's job, when done best, is to get down on both knees, lean over his children's lives, and whisper, 'Where do you want to go?'" If I could add anything to what Bob said, it would be this: make sure that every single day, you move heaven and earth to help take them to that place.

And though I'm not a mom, I've had to play one over the last couple of years, and I'm certain the above rings true for moms as well. Ask them where they want to go and move heaven and earth to take them there.

JUST DO! CHALLENGE:

What can you do tomorrow, next week, next month, or next year to ensure that you are filling their banks with amazing things? It's never too late, but don't let another day go by when you aren't making some awesome deposits. Make it a priority. You'll never look back and regret the awesome things you did, but you will certainly look back and regret the things that you failed to do. Don't wait any longer. Do the good stuff. Make the good memories. Long after you're gone, all your kids will have left of you will be memories and pictures. Make sure they're both amazing.

LESSON 6:
A PAGE IS TURNED

O ur plan from the very beginning was that we would spend just one year in the RV. Hadley would be starting Kindergarten that fall, so we figured it would be better for her reputation if her home wasn't on wheels. When we first began our adventure, we had no idea where we were going to end up. We didn't have an end destination. We just trusted that wherever God took us would be right. It's amazing looking back now how right it was. We will get back to that in a minute, but for now, let's focus on the final days in the RV.

It was bitter-sweet as these days started coming to an end. It was such an incredible chapter, and I'm pretty sure I learned more about myself, my family, and other people that year than I will for the rest of my life.

It taught us that "stuff" just doesn't really matter that much. We went from a 3000 sq. ft. house to a 40-foot motorhome, and even in that small space, we had more stuff than we could have ever needed.

In 20 years, our kids won't care if they grew up in an apartment, a mansion, or an RV. They won't care if we drove beat-up pickup trucks, minivans, or BMWs. They won't care if they wore off-brand, no-brand, or name-brand clothes. What they will care about is that we gave them a safe and loving home. A home where Jesus was always the center. A home they cherished while they were there and longed for when they were gone. Even if, for that season of our lives, our home was on wheels and was never in the same place, the kids still called it "home."

I often hear people say that they want their kids to have more in life than they had. And I appreciate that thinking. I just hope we don't get it confused and hide our own need for nice things and new stuff behind things we think our kids need. Things that, in the end, they'll probably never care about. The RV taught me that what matters most is never going to be the stuff; it's always going to be the memories that you make along the way.

That year in the RV taught us that people are going to doubt you no matter what your purpose may be. We had so many people tell us that they would never do that to their children. That they would never up-root them like we did. That the RV lifestyle isn't a realistic way to live. I promise I really care about people, but I sure didn't care what these people thought about what we were doing. I usually just smiled and thanked them for their opinion. And did my best to leave them with this idea:

It's just important for us to teach our children to live their lives full of exclamation, not full of explanation. And that's what we were doing. Every single day.

It taught us that you're never too busy to enjoy quality time with your family. You may think your life is just too hectic. But when you start thinking that way, you need to re-evaluate your priorities. Remember, your spouse, your kids, and your family aren't a distraction from the more important stuff; they *are* the more important stuff.

It taught us that tornado warnings are much more exciting when you live in an RV. When you're in a house, you have a basement, closet, or another safe room that you can retreat to. When you're in an RV, you have nowhere to go, nowhere to hide, nowhere to run. So, you just hold onto each other. You protect each other. You're with each other. It's super scary, but it's ok at the same time because once you get to the other side of it, you have a pretty awesome story to tell.

It taught us that our kids watch everything we say, everything we do, and everything we are. But at the same time, it taught us that as adults, we could learn so much from them by watching everything *they* say, everything *they* do, and everything *they* are.

It taught us that so many people are waiting for the perfect time to chase after their wildest dreams. I can't tell you how many times we heard, "We've always wanted to do that," or "I wish we could do that." It baffled me that so many people wanted to do something but were afraid to just do. We only have one life. Just one. So why aren't we running like crazy towards the things we want to do? Right now, in this moment, we are the oldest we've ever been and the youngest we'll ever be again. Stop waiting for perfect. It'll never come. Just do. And in the end, I hope and pray that you'll look back on your life with many more "I'm so glad that I did that!" moments than "I wish I would have done that!" moments.

I pray that my kids will never forget this adventure. I pray that they learned as much as I did. I pray that if they ever have a dream, they go for it. That they better never let someone tell them they can't do something. Unfortunately in life, there will always be more people telling our kids that they can't do something than there will be telling them that they can. And that's why it's important for us to be that constant voice in their ears. To be present, to show up and teach them that if they want to be superman or superwoman, no one on the planet is better equipped then they are. If they have a dream, no matter how crazy it may sound, it's our job to root them on and encourage them to go after it with everything that they are! Because if they aren't the superhero, someone else will be.

JUST DO! CHALLENGE:

On a scale from 1-10, how would you rate yourself when it comes to how well you encourage your kids to chase after the things they love? Are you building them up or breaking them down? What about you? What score would you give yourself when it comes to personally chasing after your own dreams?

I'll be honest; I was a big ol' hypocrite when it came to this for years. And it has everything to do with this book you're reading right now. I talked about and thought about writing this book for years. I wanted to do it so badly. It was so important to me and really was a dream of mine. But, like with many things in life, it just kept being pushed aside. Distractions happened. Life happened. And in our case, even death happened. It was always so important to me, and that never changed. And then, one day, I realized my kids needed to see me going after what I love. So I'm here. Not just talking about it, but doing it. And in the end, if you're lucky enough to find a way of life that you love, you must find the courage to live it!

THE
POTHOLE
SEASON

WAIT...WHERE??

The time had come to move out of the RV and into a home that didn't move. Rachel, the kids, and I had a big decision to make on where we would spend the next chapter of our lives. Throughout our marriage, Rachel and I were lucky enough to live in some pretty cool places.

We got to spend our first couple of years on the Big Island of Hawaii. Our next few years took us to East Tennessee. And it was there, in Knoxville, where we'd welcome our three kids into the world. And then, of course, we had that year cruising around in our home on wheels. But I don't even know how to tell you where we ended up next. You won't believe me. You just won't. Ok, are you ready for this? Nebraska. Yep. You read that correctly. We went from the beaches of Hawaii, to the mountains of Tennessee, to waking up to a different view each day while in the RV, to the ho-hum of Nebraska.

Before you get too judgy, let me explain Nebraska to you. If you've never been, it's an interesting place. I'm really not sure why anyone would choose to live there. Now, my Nebraska people, don't get mad just yet; I'm just giving a little backstory here. You see, I just didn't get the appeal of living there. Their winters are colder than the Arctic, and it's windy every single day. Not breezy, windy. There is a big difference. It's also super flat. There was one hill we used when we went sledding, but it was a golf course hill. It was a fake hill. It was a man-made hill. If I'm being honest, it wasn't even a hill. It was a slope.

Think about it. You don't ever hear songs about Nebraska. I mean, there's "Sweet Home Alabama," "California Girls,"

"Midnight Train to Georgia," and "Blue Hawaii." Louisiana has "Johnny B Goode," Nevada has "Viva Las Vegas," North Carolina has "Carolina in My Mind," Tennessee has "Graceland," "Walking in Memphis" and "Rocky Top." I could go on and on and on. But when it comes to Nebraska, there is nothing. Well, nothing came to mind, but as with most things in life, a quick Google search fixed that.

Bruce Springsteen sang a song called "Nebraska." But don't get excited quite yet, you crazy Nebraskans. It's about the tale of a killing spree. "From the town of Lincoln, Nebraska, with a sawed-off .410 on my lap." Need I say more?

So. Nebraska is where we ended up. Lincoln, Nebraska, to be exact. We didn't know how long we'd be there, but at least for a little while, we'd call it home. It was a new business opportunity that brought us there, but business aside, we found out pretty quickly that this was no accident and that Lincoln, Nebraska was the exact place we needed to be.

Here are my main takeaways from living in Nebraska:

1. It's the coldest place on earth. I mean it. You can try to convince me otherwise, but you'd be wrong. It's crazy how people acted out there. Some of their decisions are suspect. Like, the schools for example. They allow the kids to go out for recess as long as it's above 0. That's not normal behavior. That's child endangerment as far as I'm concerned.

    I remember one winter evening, we were leaving a basketball game and probably had about a 100-yard walk to the car. By the time we made it, all three of the kids were crying. Hadley was trying to convince me that she couldn't live here anymore. I never did quite catch what Cooper was saying; I just saw snot and tears everywhere. And poor Macklin just kept saying, "I can't feel my face, daddy. I can't feel my face." That night the wind-chill was a balmy -24°F. But that didn't seem to matter to these people, and I'm pretty sure they went outside for recess the next day.

2. It's windy all of the time. I guess it's because there is nowhere for the wind to go. It's so flat, and there is nothing to block it. So it's just always blowing. And it's super annoying. Macklin hates the wind, and I can't tell you how many times you'd find me chasing his hat down the road. To this day, anytime that we are outside, wind or not, he holds onto his hat. Talk about PTSD. I'm trying to teach him that that's not how a hat is supposed to operate, but he had a few too many traumatic, windy experiences in Nebraska to think otherwise.

3. Their food isn't very good. I love good food. And there is nothing that I ate in Lincoln that I'll miss. I know that they are known for their corn. I mean, it's everywhere. And it's in everything. It's what they do. They all husk corn. All the time. So, maybe their corn is good, but I don't eat corn. So, I won't miss their corn. There was a donut place that the kids liked, but there has never been a donut place that the kids didn't like. And I don't care for donuts, so I won't miss their donuts.

4. They have a season called "pothole season." I think it comes right as winter is becoming spring. I guess it's because their winters last for like nine months, so their roads are frozen the entire time. And once they thaw out, they pothole right up. It becomes quite the adventure to even drive a few miles. Sometimes you'll even take the long way to avoid some of the bigger holes. You must plan accordingly. When we moved there, I had no idea this was a thing. I learned it one morning in Starbucks when I overheard a few older gentlemen having a conversation about how bad the potholes were this year, and then one guy said, "And to think, it's not even pothole season yet." I mean, I just can't.

5. The people are incredible. The people made the bad food and the awful winds and the potholes and the arctic cold all worth it. I never understood why people would want to live here, but I eventually found out exactly why. The reason people were there was for the people, and though we knew that this move would be short-lived, I knew that I would miss these people. These people are so good. They cared deeply for one another.

Nebraskans love them some Nebraskans, but more than that, they welcome you like you're one of them, even if you hate their food and their weather. They make you feel right at home, even when you know you won't ever claim Nebraska as home. You hear all the time about how great people in the south are, but I'll put the Nebraskans up against anyone, anytime, anywhere. These people are some good people. These people are my kind of people.

So, Nebraska it was. We found a great condo in a great neighborhood with a great school. Our place was within walking distance of Target (Rachel's favorite feature for sure). We got plugged into an amazing church with even more amazing people. I warned everyone not to get too close to us because we wouldn't be there long. I think that was my way of making sure I didn't get too close to them. It turns out that they didn't need me, but I sure needed them. Our plan all along was to be in Nebraska for a year and then head back to Tennessee, where we would eventually settle down, for a little while at least. That was our plan. But the thing is, sometimes God has very different plans. And just when you think you have it all figured out and you're on the right path to something big, He shows up, intervenes, flips things around that don't make any sense at the time, and just says, "Nah, bigger."

LESSON 7:
"SOMETIMES, PEOPLE ARE HARD TO LOVE."

"Hey Daddy, you know how you say that we are supposed to love everybody all the time?" Hadley reluctantly asked one day on the way home from school.

"Yes, ma'am. What's up, Sweetie?" I responded, having no idea where this conversation was about to go.

"Well, did you know that sometimes, people are hard to love?" she questioned.

This stopped me dead in my tracks. And boy, was she right.

Sometimes people are super hard to love. Rachel and I had always taught our kids that they should love everybody, no matter where they are from, what they look like, what they believe, what church they attend, etc. But we never thought to teach them that sometimes people can make it really hard for us to love them. It just never crossed our minds to dive into the difficult side of love, especially at their age.

"Love Everyone" is what we have always taught our children. And it's how we strive to live our lives day in and day out. I found this ugly, messy side of love hard to explain to my six-year-old little girl. I did my best, though. I let her know that love isn't about perfection. Love is about striving to always put others before yourself. It's about being able to give of yourself and expect nothing in return. Love isn't about reciprocation, and many times you may find yourself giving it away and then wondering why. I told her that sometimes love can be super confusing, but that's never a reason not to love.

I told her that, in the end, choosing to love others will always be worth it. I told her that love has awesome power, and that by choosing to love someone, you give them a hope they may have never felt in their entire life. You give them a joy that they may not have even known existed. And you give them a sense of worth that they may have never felt before.

The fact is, love is the only reason why we are here. Because it's the exact thing that Jesus came to demonstrate to us. You want to talk about hard to love. Think about us. All of us. We aren't easy people to love. I mean, maybe you are, but I'm not. And, if we're being honest here, I bet you aren't either. Some days, we are just a mess, and we don't deserve it. Yet somehow, He still loves the heck out of us.

That's what's so cool. It doesn't matter where we come from or where we are going. He still loves us. He doesn't play favorites. He doesn't make exceptions. He just chooses to love us. Every single day. No matter how messy we may be.

So, in the end, I summed up the conversation like this; "Hadley, you're 100% right. Loving others can be super hard. But love is the only reason why we are here. Because of the love Jesus has for us. So no matter how hard it may be, there is nothing more worth spreading in the entire world."

It's so awesome how God shows up in moments like this only to prepare us for something so much bigger and better. One of our neighbors in Lincoln - let's call him Jerry because his name was Jerry - was bullied a ton at school. He was a little overweight. He was kind of awkward. He didn't speak English very well. He didn't have the coolest kicks or the nicest clothes. He was just a little different than the other kids. But man, did he have a gigantic heart, and he cared so well for people.

One day soon after the "some people are hard to love" talk I had with Hadley, the kids noticed Jerry walking toward his house, crying hysterically. They ran over to him to try and comfort him, but he wasn't having it and didn't want to talk to anyone. He just ran inside and slammed the door. Without any prompting and unbeknownst to Rachel and me, the kids decided to write Jerry a note just to let him know that they love him, that they care for him, and that they are sorry he was having a bad day.

And what happened next was beautiful. The next morning we found this letter on our front doorstep with three pieces of candy attached to it.

There are probably 100 lessons hidden in this little exchange between Jerry and the kids, but these are my biggest takeaways:

1. Be kind. Be nice. And love your neighbor. Yes, your next-door neighbor, but don't stop loving there. Love that neighbor across town, across state lines, and across the border too. You don't have to do it perfectly; that's not possible. But do as our kids and Jerry did. Simply show up and do.

Mr. Rogers was one of those people that had this figured out. And he said it best:

"Deep within us, no matter who we are, there lives a feeling of wanting to be loved and wanting to be the kind of person that others like to be with. And the greatest thing we can do is to let people know that they are loved. Love isn't a state of perfect caring. It's an active noun like 'struggle.' To love someone is to strive to accept that person exactly the way he or she is, right there and right now."[3]

2.   We can learn so much from our kids about how to love well if we just step back and watch them do life. We can learn so much from Jerry about how to love well if we just take a look at his letter. I don't know about you, but I can't remember the last time I sent a handwritten card with cool drawings telling someone how thankful I am for them. Not to mention how much I like them. Jerry's letter makes me want to be better. To do better. To send more cards to those people I care about. And maybe even draw something cool on it too. Jerry's "like letter" is a perfect reminder for us to never forget to let our people know how grateful we are for them.

3.   Jerry can draw like a bawse.

4.   I'm glad Jerry thought that Rachel and I were nice. For what it's worth, we thought he was really nice too.

It seems that at some point in our lives, we grow out of loving people the way our kids loved Jerry and the way Jerry reciprocated that love. I just wish we could figure out why that happens and somehow, someway, stop it from happening. But I'm certain that it happens because I haven't gotten a handwritten "like letter" from any of you. And I sure haven't written one either. I just think it would be pretty cool if, as adults, we loved others like this. No matter the circumstances, no matter what

[3] Fred Rogers (2006). *"Wisdom from the World According to Mister Rogers: Important Things to Remember"*

other people may think about us, totally unconditionally, just like Jerry.

This "like letter" moment and the idea that one day we grow out of loving this way brings me to a conversation that happened on a family trip we took to celebrate the first time that Rachel beat cancer. Along with Rachel and me were my brother Brian and sister-in-law Kim, my sister Taylor and brother-in-law Mike, and my cousin Morgan and his wife, Molly. I love doing life with this crew. We all have different dreams and passions. Our political views couldn't be further apart. Some of us get our news from FOX, some from CNN, and others from ESPN. We enjoy different music and different foods, and we all have different hobbies. But somehow, someway, we still love each other. We still care deeply about each other. We still show up for one another.

It was our last night of vacation, so this obviously turned into the night when we'd polish off all the wine. I mean, we couldn't fly home with it, so our only option was to drink heavily until it was gone. At the same time, this also turned into the night when we would solve all the problems of the world. I remember going around the table, making our suggestions for what we thought would make the world a better place. But we mostly focused on the United States because we were probably the most messed up and needed the most help. Now, don't get me wrong, I love our country. I'm so thankful every single day that I get to live here. And I truly do believe that we get to live in the best country in the world. That being said, it doesn't take a rocket scientist to realize that we have a ton of work to do and that we are so divided on so many things.

Some of the solutions that we came up with that evening were super far-fetched and ridiculous while some were really deep and thought-provoking. Between my cousin, who attended Dartmouth undergrad and then Harvard Law, and my brother and sister-in-law, who, along with myself, attended a college that many refer to as the Harvard of the Midwest, Mizzou, we were surrounded by greatness.

Most of the ideas that were thrown out were economically driven. There were a few that were healthcare-related, being that Rachel, Kim, and Molly all had a background in that field. But more often than not, the conversation came back to the economy and what could be done to fix things there. I'm not going to get into the specifics because much of what was discussed was way over my head. But if you're interested, my cousin wrote a book about money, and the financial crisis, and a bunch of stuff like that. I think he sold about 12 copies because only 12 people in the world could understand it. But I'm proud of him for doing it; I'm just not going to read it.

All that to say, when it was my turn to take a crack at the "How do we fix this?" question, my answer was simple, "We just need to love people better." I shared with them the story of Jerry and our kids and explained if we'd just show love this way, we'd be in a much better place. I explained to them that I realized that the kids loving Jerry this way didn't immediately change the world, but it did immediately change his world. And sometimes that's enough.

I won't mention who said it, but someone at the table that night referred to this idea as "cute." They then continued to explain that we live in a country where very few would adopt this stance, so it was only a pipe dream. That only a select few would care for those that have no one to care for them. Only a handful would encourage and uplift those that needed it. And that being kind to others is just a ton to ask from a ton of people. But it was a cute idea.

They made it very clear that the majority of us are just too selfish to care for anyone but ourselves. And sadly, they were right. But at the same time, I like to think that it wouldn't hurt for the minority to go out and try our best. I think the ripple effect of us truly caring for people, encouraging them, believing in them, and simply showing up in love for them could be pretty awesome. I guess what I'm saying is that I believe it's worth a shot. And as far as I know, loving others better is the only solution that I have right this second that I can be a part of and actually see change. Maybe not change for the whole world, but change for someone's world.

I can think of a million times that I didn't deserve to be loved, especially by Rachel and the kids, yet they continued to show up and love me anyway. Times I lost my patience. Times I was super annoyed and raised my voice. Times I wasn't fully present. Times I was too competitive in sports, in business, or in life. Yet, for some reason, they just continued to show up for me. I guess the truth is that, in the end, that's what loves is supposed to do. It doesn't look for a formal invite or a huge reason; it just shows up. It's not looking to be recognized or for anything in return. It just shows up. Even when it's hard, and it's the last thing it feels like doing, love just relentlessly shows up. And if we're really lucky, it may even come with candy, just like Jerry's did.

JUST DO! CHALLENGE:

I want to take the pressure off and remind you that we can't do this perfectly. Only Jesus can do that. So don't try to do it perfectly. But I do think that we can all do it a little better. What little changes can we make today that may just cause a big change in someone's life? What about a little more gratitude when you get your coffee this morning? What about taking a little more interest in someone's day today? The doorman, the janitor, the drive-thru worker, the gas station attendant, the bank teller, etc. What about emailing your team at work and just letting them know you are grateful for them? What about a handwritten "like letter" to a friend letting them know you're thinking of them? What about a quick pit stop on the way home so you can grab some flowers or something special for your spouse? Not because it's an occasion. Not because you're looking for anything in return. There doesn't need to be a reason or an explanation. With love, there doesn't need to be a "because."

LESSON 8:
"I DON'T THINK I'M THE SMARTEST."

My parents weren't the parents that pushed me super hard in school. I mean, they cared and wanted me to do well, but they seemed to understand that what was happening in grade school social studies probably wasn't going to make or break the person I'd become one day. Needless to say, I did just enough to get by, and though I was never the smartest kid in class, I was always the fastest. Not the fastest at getting my work done. That wasn't important to me. The fastest, as in I could run the fastest. That was my claim to fame at Winship Elementary, and to be honest, being the fastest may not have gotten me that far in life, but it got me super far in elementary school. Whether it was the mile run, the 40-yard dash, or the shuttle run, everyone else knew that they were fighting for second place.

I share this with you not to brag, although I know you're impressed. I share this because of something Cooper shared with me one day after school that I could so relate to. She told me, "Daddy, I know I'm not the smartest kid in class, but I think that I'm the best dancer. And I'm pretty sure I'm the happiest."

I don't know that I've ever had a prouder moment in my life as a dad. It had nothing to do with the fact that she didn't think that she was the smartest, and though I was super impressed, it wasn't the fact that she was the best dancer either. I mean, that's cool and is kind of like me being the fastest, which y'all can obviously see I've hung onto for many years. But the part that made me the proudest was the happiest part.

You see, ever since I was a little kid, I've lived by this rule in my life that I refer to as the "Law of Happy." This law states that if I wake up two days in a row and I'm not happy doing what I'm doing, then I stop doing it. It's that simple. Now don't get me wrong; there are things that I do in my day that don't bring me a ton of joy. Things like vacuuming and mowing the lawn. But guess what, I don't do them two days in a row. I don't know where I picked this law up. I'm assuming it was introduced to me by my parents. But as far back as I can remember, this is how I've lived my life. That being said, Mom and Dad, thank you for teaching me this. Of all the laws there are, this is by far one of my favorites.

I don't ever want to build something into my life that causes me to be unhappy. I mean, none of us want to do that, but I feel that far too many of us have allowed it to happen. I'm just here to tell you that I don't want that for me, for my kids, or for you. I may not even know you, and we may never meet in person, but I sure don't want you to live a life where you wake up unhappy. If I've learned anything over the last few years and all that our family went through, it's that life is way too short to live even one more day that way.

Please understand that I'm not telling you to go quit your job today. I don't need husbands and wives calling and telling me that their spouse read my book, decided they were unhappy and quit their job or their marriage, or stopped paying the mortgage, or got their car repossessed. I'm not saying be irresponsible. I'm saying be happy. Don't do things over and over that make you unhappy. It's a vicious cycle, and trust me, just on the other side of your unhappiness is happiness. It's so close. It's right there. And as parents, one of our most important roles should be to encourage our kids to go for happy. But how can we encourage it if we aren't going for it as well? Hence, me finally finishing this book.

You see, like my parents, Rachel and I were never the parents to push our kids in school. Yes, I'd like them to pass. Yes, I'd like them to have a good work ethic and want them to do the best that they can. But that's not what's most important. More than anything, I want them to be respectful and kind to their teachers, their friends, and anyone else they come into contact with. And I want them to be happy.

Now that I think about it, I probably spend more time encouraging Cooper in her dance than I do in her math. And the reason for that is because dancing makes Cooper happy. It's her thing, and it's what she loves to do. She does it all day, every day, everywhere we go, and that makes her happy. Which makes me happy.

Let me be clear; I'm not saying that we shouldn't care about our kids' schooling. But I am saying that I think some of us care way too much about it. My challenge here is pretty simple. Some of us just need to stop pushing so hard, especially with things that don't bring joy into our children's lives. This isn't just school related. Some of us push our kids too hard in sports, and what inevitably happens is that they get burned out. Why? Because it's not fun anymore. I just want to encourage you to help your kids find things they love (even if it's not what you love) and spend time with them in that thing. Build them up, encourage the heck out of them, and spend more time and resources on that thing because that thing brings them joy.

For some kids, that may be school. Hadley loves school. She gets a kick out of complex math equations and spelling words she's never heard before. When she's not in school, she wants to play school. When she's not challenged in her day, she's annoyed. School makes Hadley happy. School brings her joy. She's super gifted, and for her, being the smartest means something. And I love her for that. So I'll encourage her every single day with her schoolwork. I'll get excited and geek out about spelling tests and science projects with her. I don't understand it, but I love it. Because she loves it. And because that's what makes her happy.

It's actually quite funny to see how different Hadley and Cooper feel about school. They are literally just like my brother and me. My brother was always the smartest. He didn't have to try very hard in school, and a 4.0 was just what he did. And most times, he had even more than a 4.0, which I never quite understood. How do you get better than perfect? I didn't pay a ton of attention to it because that wasn't my thing, but I'm pretty sure he had like a 4.25 GPA or something like that. I think he probably has his GPA tattooed somewhere on his body. School just came easy to him. And he enjoyed it. I don't get it, but it doesn't matter because he did.

That wasn't the case for me. I had to work my butt off to keep a 3.0 GPA and never sniffed that 4.0 number. It took me a lot longer than the average person to finish a paper or an exam. I had to ask for help a lot. I had to spend more time than the average person doing whatever it was that we were doing. School never came easy to me, and I really didn't enjoy it much. I loved going to class, I loved my teachers, and I loved my friends, but the learning part didn't do anything for me. I did just enough to get by and earn a degree. Then forgot all that I had learned, and I've never used any of it again.

I mean, I took Spanish for two full years, and to this day, the only thing I can say is "Tengo que ir al baño." Which means, "I have to go to the bathroom." The only reason I knew this is because Spanish class followed lunch each day, and I have the world's smallest bladder. Our teacher insisted we speak Spanish while in class, so I spent much of my two years raising my hand and telling my teacher that I had to pee.

I'm not an expert on birth order, but I do think it's interesting that Cooper is a middle child like me, and Hadley is the oldest, like her Uncle Brian. Coop and I are a lot alike, and Hadley and her Uncle Brian are cut from the same cloth. And then there are my nephews (Brian and Kim's kids.) They have five total but two boys. Tyler is the oldest and just like his daddy and Hadley. Grayson is the middle, and he's a lot like Cooper and me.

I remember a conversation with Grayson on a trip we recently took to visit their family in Seattle. Remember, Brian is the smart one. He is a big shot at Microsoft and is changing the world when it comes to energy and stuff like that. I'm super proud of what he's doing and blessed to get to call him my brother. He's been on CNN, Squawk Box, and other shows that come on stations that those of us that get our news from ESPN don't really ever watch. I told him I was impressed, but when he makes the Top 10 on SportsCenter, that's when he will really have my attention.

Ok, back to the conversation. Grayson was talking about how he had to work super hard in school and how things don't come as easily to him as they do to his brother. That he must spend hours and hours on his homework and that it's just not a ton of fun for him. I explained to him that he sounds a lot like Cooper and me and that he's going to be just fine because he's "people smart."

Grayson stopped me as I was talking and said, "Uncle Brandon," I could see he was still gathering his thoughts before saying, "That sounds good, but who has gone further, you or my dad?"

Mind you, we were having this conversation in Brian and Kim's newly remodeled kitchen, in their beautiful big ol' home, with stunning million-dollar views. And at that time, Rachel and I were renting a three-bedroom condo that wasn't much to brag about. Their kitchen was larger than our entire place. So from the outside looking in, and from a ten-year-old perspective, his dad had for sure gone much further.

After some quick self-reflection, I responded, "Man, I think we've both gone far. Your dad has done and continues to do amazing things in the world. It's really impressive to watch what he's doing. But more than that, he gets to come home to y'all each night. A family that loves and supports each other with all the ups and downs that life has to offer. A family that helps others even before helping themselves. A family that looks out for each other and always has each other's backs. A family that puts Jesus first in all that they do. And you know what, buddy, that's how I see my family too. No, our house isn't as big as y'alls. No, our bank account doesn't have as many numbers in it as your parents does. And no, I don't have a fancy title at a fancy company like your dad. But I'm super happy, just like your dad. Both of our families have everything in the world we need and so much more. And neither of us would change a dang thing."

Grayson thought for a second and eventually replied, "You know what, Uncle Brandon, you're right. I am going to go really far, just like you."

Grayson and Cooper are two of the most likable humans I know, and they are so much fun to be around. They light up any room they walk into and always leave a situation better than when they found it. They are both super encouraging and care so much for others. They are both so kind and talented. And they are so dang funny. You cannot be in a room with them without smiling. They will both do some big things in the world, and they will both go really far. There is a good chance that neither Grayson, Cooper, nor I will run the Microsoft energy department as Brian does. We may never be a top executive at Amazon, Apple, or Google. And it really is too bad for all of those companies, because Grayson and Cooper are the types of people that I'd choose to run my company every single time. They are the types of people that you want to surround yourself with in life. They show up for people. They are the kind of people that can and will create something amazing wherever it is that they choose to go.

The point of all of this is that sometimes we need to stop pushing our kids into the wrong things. Sometimes I think we push them at things that we care more about than they do. We push them because our parents pushed us or maybe because our parents didn't, and we are trying to make up for it in some strange way. We push them at things that are more important to our reputation than theirs. We are pushers, and all too often, we push them in the wrong way.

The scary thing is that as adults, we have the tendency to push ourselves in the wrong things. We spend so much time focusing on the things we think matter much more than they actually do. And I think this can turn into a vicious and scary cycle.

I'm reminded of a girl I dated in high school. Not really the girl, but her mom. They had this room in their house; it was just to the right of the front door as you entered their home. You couldn't miss it. It was beautiful. It stood out because it looked so different from the rest of the house. It had this pretty white carpet that had never been stepped on by a human foot. Well, maybe a human foot, but never a human foot in a human shoe. I promise you, a foot with a shoe on it had never entered that room. It was perfectly vacuumed daily and looked like it was professionally done by the same people that mow the grass at football stadiums. Each day, the carpet had these Instagram-worthy manicured lines. It seemed to me that her number one goal in life was to keep that room perfect. To make sure there was never a footprint on that carpet. I never understood why, but she was dead set on humans never entering that room. I always wanted to touch it with my foot. I wanted to see what would happen. I wondered what it felt like. I was super tempted but never did because I feared the repercussions.

The thing is that for as long as I dated her daughter, the mom hit her goal. She succeeded. That carpet was perfect. That room was pristine. No shoe had ever touched it, and very few humans had ever had the privilege to enter it. I don't know this for a fact, but I bet if I was able to ask her mom today, she would regret that she cared so much about that room. I bet she'd regret that she spent so much time, so much energy, and so much effort on that room. But from the outside looking in, that room was her pride and joy. And I know that it made her very happy. But I bet she would admit today that she may have been focused on the wrong thing. I bet she would give anything to be able to go back to those days and have memories of kids running through that room with muddy feet and spilled sodas. I bet today she wishes that room would have been a playroom, not a showroom. She spent so much of her time focused on that room. She absolutely hit her goal of keeping it perfect. But in the end, I wonder if she had the wrong goal. Because all that was left were memories of a super clean carpet and a space no one was ever welcome to enter.

Disclaimer: I loved her mom, and she was terrific. She was so kind and treated me so well. She was actually very welcoming, but we just weren't welcome in that room. I just never understood the room; that's all.

As a parent, maybe I shouldn't be so proud of Cooper for not being the smartest. But I am. Because that just doesn't matter to her. And she's the happiest kid I know. And, like Cooper, I'm not the smartest, but I too, am happy. I do what I love to do every day. I have three precious, healthy children that I get to meet at the bus stop each afternoon. I have an incredible family that loves us all so well. I have some of the most amazing friends in the world who would literally lay down their lives for my kids or me. I guess you could say that I'm a collector of happiness. Every day that goes by, I do my best to collect all the great things that happen. I'm not saying that everything is perfect, but I'm not a person that spends a ton of time focusing on the negative or the things that are out of my control. I just continue to do my best each day to live by the "Law of Happy."

JUST DO! CHALLENGE:

Are you happy? Loaded question, I know. But I'm serious, are you? Are you pushing your kids or yourself to be great in the wrong things? How much will the "showroom" - those things that you obsess over - really matter in 20 years? Sometimes achieving the goal doesn't matter if the goal was wrong to begin with. If you're going to be a pusher, be a happiness pusher. Push happiness on your children, your family, and all others that you encounter. And don't neglect yourself. Do what makes you happy. Do it every single day. You'll never regret it. If it's dancing, dance. If it's singing, sing. If it's acting, act. If it's school, go back to school. If it's energy stuff, do energy stuff. If it's working on cars, work away. If we could all just be happiness pushers, imagine how the world would change. And I've got the perfect people to lead that world. Grayson and Cooper, you're up.

LESSON 9:
"I LIKE WHEN THE SUN IS IN MY EYES."

I remember as a kid, each summer, our family would pile into the car and hit the road for our annual trip to Florida. I loved all the memories we made there, but I hated the drive with a passion. I'm not sure that there was anything in life I disliked more than sitting in the back seat of a car between my brother and sister for 12 straight hours. Whether you're heading out for a quick three-hour trip or in for the long haul on a 12-hour excursion, it becomes way too long within the first 20 minutes. And then it begins.

> *"Are we there yet?"*
> *"Daddy, I need to pee."*
> *"Mommy, I'm hungry."*
> *"I'm soooooo hot."*
> *"Daddy, can I take my shoes off?"*
> *"I'm soooooo thirsty."*
> *"Mommy, my feet are so cold."*
> *"When are we going to be there?"*
> *"Daddy, I need to pee again."*
> *"Mommy, can we watch a movie?"*
> *"This is soooooo boring."*
> *"Mommy, Sis won't stop copying me."*
> *"Not that movie, Daddy. We've already seen this."*
> *"Daddy, I have to pee right now. It's starting to come out."*
> *"Mommy, Sis doesn't want to play with me."*

"Daddy, my iPad is dead."
"But when are we going to be there?"
"Daddy, I think I just peed my pants."

And my favorite of all time and where we will learn our next lesson; *"Daddy, the sun is in my eyes."*

I'm sure my parents would be the first to say that I was guilty of saying all these things during our family road trips. I think it's safe to say that every parent throughout the history of time that ever took a road trip can relate to some or all of these things. And now that I'm the parent, the one that gets me every time is the "sun in the eyes" one. I mean, what are we supposed to do about that? If you need to pee, I can stop. Need your iPad, no worries. Want a different movie on? I got you. Are your feet cold? Here's a blanket.

But the "sun in your eyes" one, what the heck would you like me to do? I usually just say something along the lines of, "Sorry, it'll be over soon." But in those rare times when you know you're approaching an upcoming turn and the sun will no longer be in their eyes, you get to be the hero. A simple, "Hold, please. Let me move the sun for you," and then you do your thing. At that moment, my kids believed I could actually move the sun. It's not that I'm playing God here. It's that I'm playing Super Dad, who happens to be able to move the sun on occasion. The issue is that more often than not, when I move it, it goes into someone else's eyes, so we are in the same predicament all over again. So it becomes cool and then uncool almost simultaneously.

On one particular road trip, when for some reason, Rachel had to fly to meet us, I was given the task of driving the kids from Kansas City, Missouri, to Knoxville, Tennessee, all on my own. Oh, and it needed to be done in one day. We hadn't been on the road for 10 minutes when the questions, demands, and requests began. I told them that if they would just be patient and watch eight movies, we'd be there. That's it. Just eight movies, and we are in Knoxville. I thought that was great logic. They didn't seem to grasp it.

I could give you all the boring details of this trip and fill you in on each of the 27 pit stops we had to make along the way, but I'll leave that for another book and another time. Fast forward about nine hours into this trip, when somehow the sun was in the exact right place to be in all of our eyes at the exact same time. I'm not even sure how that's possible, but everyone seemed to be going blind. Hadley and Cooper were not ok. They were both on the verge of tears. It was making a long day even longer, and they were begging me to use my superpowers to move the sun. Unfortunately, we were on a stretch on I-24 when there wouldn't be a single turn for about 75 miles. My dad powers just didn't matter at that moment.

It was so bad, and they were so annoyed that I contemplated pulling off the interstate as soon as I found a place. But then, out of nowhere, after nine hours in the car, Macklin, who was four at the time, with the sun beaming into his little blue eyes, said, "Daddy, I like when the sun is in my eyes. It keeps my seat warm."

Perspective. I mean, I think we can all agree that no one likes the sun in their eyes. Never have I ever heard of someone enjoying that. Or finding the positive in that. Not until a four-year-old showed me how to turn even the worst of childhood problems into something positive. A solar-powered seat warmer. I long for Mack's childlike perspective.

As adults, we often talk about childlike faith and how awesome it is. How we all need a little more of that type of faith in our daily lives. And I couldn't agree more. Just the other day, out of the blue, as Macklin and I were playing catch, he said, "Daddy, it's ok if I die before you because God will play catch with me until you get to Heaven." I have no idea where he gets this stuff, but he's so right, and I want to live my life with a faith like that.

Rachel and I did our best, and I continue to do my best to teach our children that they can be anything in the world that they want to be. The problem is that as adults, we often neglect to believe this about ourselves. Somewhere along the way, we have lost faith in ourselves, in others, and in our situation. We are afraid to try something new because it'll hurt if we fall. And even worse, people may see us fall, and we wouldn't want that to happen. Yet, at the same time, we encourage our kids to try and try again, knowing that if they fall, they will bounce right back up and give it another shot. I don't know about you, but as I read that out loud, it just sounds a little hypocritical to me.

I love watching my kids and how they live their days with that childlike faith, and I think that as adults, we could all learn a ton if we could somehow view our days through that same lens. At the same time, wouldn't it be awesome if we took it a step further and added a childlike perspective?

The perspective that the sun in your eyes just means you have a super awesome and super powerful seat warmer.

The perspective that mommies really are superheroes and can do so many things that dads can't do. Like, heal boo-boos with the magic of a kiss. And make five different meals, for five different people, with five different requests, and have them all ready at the exact same time.

The perspective that if you don't wipe that kiss off your cheek that you get in the morning, you can take it with you all day long.

The perspective that coloring outside the lines is always more fun and will likely turn into a masterpiece well before it would if you followed the rules and stayed between the lines.

The perspective that there is no good reason at all that clothes need to match. And that rocking black and white polka dot leggings with a rainbow stripe shirt just works. And it works really well.

The perspective that making your bed really doesn't matter that much. You're just going to get back in it in a few hours anyway.

The perspective that vegetables just suck. And that even Popeye didn't eat his spinach until he absolutely had to.

I just think it would be super cool if we, as adults, had a little bit more childlike perspective. Because in the end, clothes don't *really* need to match, and beds don't *really* need to be made. What we all need instead is more kisses that can heal. And the understanding that coloring outside the lines is just more fun.

What if, as adults, we were just more curious? I don't know about your kids, but mine can ask me 1,000 questions, and once those are answered, they are ready with 1,000 more. Curiosity opens doors and spurs imagination. Kids can learn to grow and become their own people by simply asking questions. Why have we stopped asking questions? At what age did we decide that we knew enough and didn't need to learn more? What would happen if we just became curious again? I think what would happen is that we'd sit back and watch the world open itself up to us like we'd forgotten was even possible.

What if, as adults, we just lived our lives with more excitement? I don't know about your kids, but mine can get excited about anything. Everything we do is a new adventure, a new opportunity to explore, and a new way to see the world. I'm afraid that, as adults, we are just doing what we can to make it to the weekend. We just go through the motions to get through our day, just to do it all over again the next day. Nothing is exciting about what we do because we have the same routine, see the same people, and do the same things day in and day out.

What if tomorrow we just switched things up a little bit? Nothing major, but what if we just took a different route to work? Maybe we'd see something new. What if we stopped at a different coffee shop and actually went inside instead of driving through? Maybe we'd meet a new smiling face, or perhaps be that smiling face for someone that needs it. What if we got really crazy and ate at a new restaurant that we'd never tried? And we ordered food that we'd never heard of? I feel like if we could just change our routine, then our perspective would change right along with it.

What if, as adults, we lived our lives with a little bit more wonder? I don't know about your kids, but mine are amazed by something new every 30 seconds. I'm not sure why, I'm not sure how, but according to them, everything has some awesome to it. At some point in our adult lives, we stopped having that sense of wonder. We are no longer impressed with the beauty of the things around us and how blessed we truly are. We are so focused on looking down at our phones that we forget to look up and see all the wonder that God has created around us. Imagine for a minute a day without your phone. I know that some of you probably just threw up in your mouth a little bit. Trust me, I'm as guilty as anyone when it comes to phone time. It's the first thing we grab for in the morning and the last thing we check before we go to bed. I just wonder how many cool things we've missed, how many amazing encounters have been lost, and how much more wonder we'd have if we just put the phone down and took a look around. I bet what we'd find is that this world we live in is pretty dang cool. I bet we'd imagine and wonder a bit more. I bet we'd be more grateful for all that God is doing all around us, all of the time.

What if, as adults, we started to live our lives today, forgetting about yesterday? I don't know about your kids, but if my kids' day doesn't go as planned, they still wake up the next day with a blank canvas. In their minds, there is no reason to worry about what happened yesterday because they can't go back to it. And sometimes I think we forget that we can't either. Every day invites a new, fresh start to learn more, to discover more, to play more, and to grow more. Let's work on forgetting about yesterday because if we don't, we may miss out on the amazing things God is doing in our lives today.

What if we not only lived forgetting about yesterday, but we also lived not worrying so much about tomorrow? I don't know about your kids, but mine live so much for today and in the current moment that they can't even think about tomorrow. They savor the now. They take it all in. They have no time to worry about what's to come. As adults, for some reason, we spend so much of our time worrying about tomorrow that we forget to enjoy the awesomeness that surrounds today.

What if we just remembered that it's ok to slow down once in a while? I don't know about your kids, but mine are never in a hurry. I mean, never. They truly take the time to stop and smell the roses, or play with the worms, or collect the cool rocks. All the roses. All the worms. And all the rocks. They take the time to enjoy the beauty around them, and the only way to do that is to actually slow down and see it. When did we stop noticing the million little miracles happening all around us every single day? All too often, as adults, we forget to soak in the current moment because we are too busy focusing on the next moment. Try something new this week. Actually stop and smell the roses; I bet you haven't done that in years.

What if we only spent our time doing things that brought us joy? I don't know about your kids, but if mine don't enjoy doing something, they don't do it. I'm not saying they enjoy doing chores or things like that, but I mean things that they have a choice in. My kids spend their days doing what they love most, and they do it with passion. They don't waste their time on things that don't make them happy. When did we stop pursuing things that we are passionate about? I said it earlier, and I'll say it again – go find something that you love, do that every single day for the rest of your life, and watch as the world changes right around you.

What if we were just more fearless? I don't know about your kids, but mine go through their lives with the kind of courage that makes me nervous every single day. They jump off things that are way too high. They ride their bikes way too fast. They wrestle way too rough. They just go for it with a nothing-to-lose type attitude. And 99.9% of the time, it turns out awesome. What if we lived our lives like our children do, understanding that the only thing to lose by not going for it is a chance to learn something extraordinary?

What if we were all willing to just forgive more freely? I don't know about your kids, but mine forgive me way quicker than I probably deserve. It's amazing how a simple hug and an I'm sorry can turn a bad decision into a good lesson. Somehow they understand that a bad moment doesn't make a bad human. I think it would be awesome if, as adults, we understood that too. Unfortunately, we like to hold onto grudges. I've talked to countless families that have been torn apart because of that thing called pride and people not being willing to ask for forgiveness. People not being willing to say, "I'm sorry."

It's sad to think about the cousins that didn't get to know each other because of this. The aunts and uncles who didn't know their nieces and nephews because of this. The in-laws who don't have a relationship with their grandkids because of this stubbornness that so many of us have. If nothing else comes from this entire book, I hope someone will pick up the phone and call that person that they've been feuding with for years and just say, "I'm sorry." If you won't do it for yourself, do it for your kids. We tell our kids to never go to bed angry with anyone and to always ask for forgiveness before they close their eyes. We didn't make this rule up; Jesus did.

JUST DO! CHALLENGE:

I'm so grateful that Mack taught me the "sun in my eyes" perspective. As dads, moms, grandparents, uncles, aunts, or just adults in general, we should all strive to have more of a childlike perspective. And not be so quick to correct a perspective that may be very different from the way we see things. It's easy to jump to the "right way" or the only way we know, when often, letting our kids see things from their perspective ends up revealing a much more beautiful perspective, not just for them but for all of us. What can you let go of today? Let it go. Who do you need to call? Make the call. What are you anxious about that you can set free? This is your permission to set it free. What questions do you have for people? Ask 'em. What would you really love to do that you're just so afraid of? Just Do!

LESSON 10:
QUANTITY TIME > QUALITY TIME

It was one of those weeks when I was just a super sucky dad. This happens way more than I like to admit, but for some reason, this week, I just felt the suckiness even more than usual. We had just returned from a super fun but super tiring family trip to the Northwest. And the moment we stepped off the plane, it began to happen. First, it was Hadley, then Cooper, and then Macklin. The flu bug had come and didn't have plans to leave any of us alone.

I had a really important business trip coming up, so getting sick was not an option. Unfortunately, because we were gone the week before, Rachel was scheduled to work a bunch which left me to play nurse to the flu-infested kids. I think I'm a pretty ok dad, but you'll never hear me claim to be an ok nurse. In fact, I'm a terrible nurse. I don't do snot, I don't do fevers, I don't do diarrhea, and I for sure don't do puke. If I see puke or even hear puke, I puke. No question about it. And there is simply no way to avoid it.

I wish I wasn't like this. I hate that puke is my biggest fear in life. Most of y'all probably fear public speaking or death, but not me. I fear puke. This causes a huge problem when the kids are sick because I care about them so much, and I'm willing to do whatever it takes to care for them until puke happens. That's where the line is drawn for me. I'm embarrassed to admit this, but when you puke, you're on your own. Remember when I mentioned that God spent a little more time when he made moms? I think this was one of the powers that He gave them that

He didn't give dads. I mean, maybe some dads have this power, but this dad doesn't. I hate to admit it, but I've come to terms with the fact that I just wasn't made to be a great caretaker in times like these.

Man, I'm glad God made mommies. Not just for times of puke, but in all the other times too. That being said, when puke happens, I do find myself being extra thankful to the Big Guy for making mommies the way that He did. I don't want to harp on this puke stuff too much longer, but I remember the year when the kids got hit with pretty hard with the flu. It was about midnight one night when Cooper came strolling into our room and laid down next to me. This was normal behavior for Coop, so I didn't think much of it at the time. She would typically "sneak" into our room between midnight and 2 a.m. and climb into bed with us. When I say "sneak," there was nothing sneaky about the way she would enter. She liked to make it known that she was there. By kicking, elbowing, climbing, snoring, and drooling all over us.

On this particular night, she decided to make her presence known on an entirely different level. She hadn't been lying there for five minutes when it happened. Puke. Everywhere. Not just a little bit. I'm talking projectile vomit. I immediately went into panic mode, which essentially meant I did nothing but tried to avoid puking myself. At the same time, Rachel went into supermom mode. Which looked a lot like a counselor, MD, personal assistant, janitor, RN, life coach, and a bunch of other incredible professions, all wrapped into one. And if y'all think the only person she was tending to was Cooper, you must have missed it earlier when I told y'all that I fear puke more than anything in this world. She not only had to deal with a puking Coop, but she also had to make sure that I was doing ok as well. And she did. I'm telling you. Mommies are different.

Fast forward to about 2:30 a.m. By this point, I had retreated to Hadley's room and was sleeping on her floor because, well, you heard what happened in our room. As I was just getting settled after experiencing one of the most traumatic events of my entire life, it happened. Again. Puke. Everywhere. Not just a little bit. I'm talking explosive vomit. Guys, this was not a drill. This was actually happening. It was now Hadley's turn. And this time, I wasn't able to flee fast enough. I got puked on.

What I'm about to say may sound dramatic to you, but at that moment, at least for a split second, I believe I remember asking Jesus to go ahead and bring me home. I no longer wanted to be here. Not under these conditions. As I snapped out of my plea to Jesus, I saw Rachel swoop in like a thief in the night and whisk Hadley away.

What happened next was all a blur, but as she rushed Hadley into the bathroom, I heard Coop start again. At this point, I'm just dry-heaving and on the verge of passing out. But out of nowhere, something came over me, and I sprang into action. Well, kind of. I ran into our room and held Cooper's hair back with one hand while holding my nose with the other. So now the girls were going puke-for-puke with one another. Coop was crying and scared because being scared is normal when you get sick at five years old. Hadley was crying and scared because her perfect attendance record was now going to be in jeopardy. Rachel was comforting them both simultaneously and assured Hadley that missing a day of kindergarten won't cause her to fall short of becoming valedictorian.

After things had calmed down a bit, Rachel proceeded to rip the sheets off Hadley's bed. Started another load of laundry. Scrubbed the puke off the floor. Continued to comfort the girls. Held hair back when it was needed. Scratched backs. Proactively laid towels out around the beds. Gathered puke buckets. And a million other little things. All while I just sat in shock about what just went down. About what I had just endured. I have no idea what the next few hours looked like that night. Rachel was with the girls. I was downstairs on the couch at that point. I'm pretty sure I slept for the next few hours. And I'm pretty sure that Rachel didn't.

Now back to where we began. That time when Super Rachel wasn't there to assist in the outbreak of sickness that was happening all around me. Snot and used tissues covered the entire house. So many coughs and sneezes. Germs were so evident that you could actually see them. People say that you can't see germs, but I beg to differ. They were seen in my house that week. They were everywhere, they were obvious, and they were relentless.

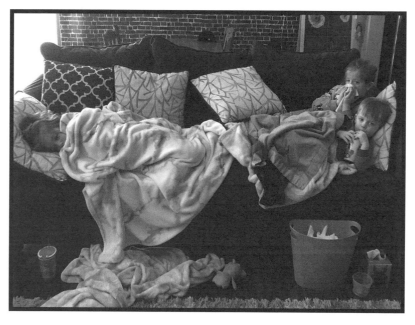

I did the best that I could that week. I tried to be the caretaker that my kids needed. I was there to refresh their Sprites®. I was there to clean up the used tissue mounds they'd built on the floors. I was there to wipe noses and to give them their medicine. And I was even there to make them soup and grilled cheese when they needed to be fed. But even while doing all of those amazing things, I realized I was lacking in many other areas. I wasn't the best cuddler. Rachel always cuddled them when they were sick. I didn't do that. I didn't nurture them the way their mommy would have. I wasn't the best encourager. I wasn't even close to the best nurse. I'm not even sure anyone would have classified me as a nurse that week. To be honest, I did as little as I possibly could. I just kept them alive and then did my best to avoid them the rest of the time. I didn't want what they had. I had things to do. Places to be. People to see.

I got the kids down at about 6:30 p.m. on the evening before I was to leave town for a few days. I mean, that's pretty impressive in and of itself. It may have been drug-induced, but either way, they were all sound asleep by 7. I was hoping for a good night's sleep that night, but between all of the coughing and sneezing and snoring, sleep just wasn't in the cards. By 3:30 a.m., I'd given up on the idea of getting any more sleep, and decided it was best to go ahead and start getting ready. About 15 minutes later, Hadley and her snotty nose walked into the bathroom where I was. I just assumed she had to pee because why else would she be up at 3:45 a.m.? Turns out she didn't have to pee. She walked right over to me and gave me a big hug. Then

she started sobbing. Out of control, big ol' tears, snot all over my pants and my shirt, bawling. I couldn't get any words out of her at first, so I chalked it up to a bad dream. After a few minutes of hugging and me asking her what was wrong, she calmed down a bit and told me that she was just really sad that I was leaving. That she really wished I didn't have to go and that she was just going to miss me so much.

We hugged and hugged and hugged. She cried and cried and cried. And the truth is that I may have cried a little bit too. After getting it all out, I tucked her back into her bed, kissed her on the forehead, and told her that I'd be back in three dark rests and that I loved her so much.

As I was driving to the airport, something hit me. I'd been a dad for six years at that point, and up until that morning, I had assumed that quality time with our kids mattered most. But that interaction with Hadley made me realize that I may have had it all wrong. She made me realize that maybe it's simply time that matters the most. Just being there. To wipe snot. To clean up used tissues. To refill Sprites®. To hug. And to hug. And to hug. And to cry sometimes too.

See, I felt like such a sucky dad that entire week, but according to them, I was there. I may not have been on the same couch. I may not have even been in the same room most of the time. But I was there. I was far from perfect. But I was there. And being there was all that mattered to them.

Our kids don't think in terms of quality time; they think in terms of quantity time. They just want to know that we are there when they look up. The fact is, it's not easy to orchestrate quality time. Especially as our kids grow older. So instead of putting all the pressure on ourselves to plan these quality times that may not even come together, how about we pursue planning quantity times? These times aren't meant to be perfect, but if we plan enough of these times, quality will inevitably come. We should be doing all we can to plan quantity times and then watch for all the quality moments that come from them.

Ok, I've said all of that, and now I'm going to contradict myself a little. Remember when Hadley asked me if I loved my phone more than I loved her? Gosh, I still wish I could take that moment away. But anyway, it was obvious to her because I spent more time on it than I did with her. At that moment, she was begging me for quality. Yes, I was there. Yes, when she looked, she saw me. But she was seeing me look at the wrong thing. She just wanted to see my face. Let's not make our kids beg for quality. Whenever quality presents itself during quantity, we need to make darn sure we are ready for it.

So the next time your kids are begging for your attention. The next time they want you to watch them do the same trick they've been doing for the last two years, that really isn't a trick at all. The next time they want to show you their cartwheel or their handstand. The next time they say "Daddy" or "Mommy, watch this." Do me a favor and put down your phone. Put down the iPad. Stop scrolling through social media. Stop cooking dinner for a second. Pause the show. And watch them. Watch them with your whole face.

In the end, our kids don't just remember the "special times," but instead, they simply remember all the times. Just being there is the most important place we can be. The safety, the comfort, the security of them being able to call for Daddy or Mommy and for us to be there to reply is enough.

JUST DO! CHALLENGE:

Time matters. All time matters. What small changes can you make in your schedule today to be there more? Not next week. Not next month. Not next quarter. Today. I don't know about you, but I've been guilty of "playing busy" more than my fair share of times. I've hidden in my office, scrolling through social media or lost on some YouTube rabbit trail. I'm guilty. And to be honest, some days I'm just spent and don't have the energy to give anything else to anyone else. This is your friendly reminder that you don't have to entertain; you just have to be. It doesn't have to be quality; because with quantity, quality just shows up. And it may even show up in the form of a flu-infested, snotty six-year-old when you least expect it.

LESSON 11:
"I'LL GO AS BATMAN!"

Macklin had a big ol' crush. At the time, he was in pre-school, and she was in 5th grade. Each afternoon at 2:53 p.m., Macklin would be found just outside the doors of his sisters' school waiting, not to see them, but to see her. And each day, he would get super flustered and turn bright red when she'd walk out. Often, he would have to run away because he couldn't contain himself. And every day, it was so awesome to watch how he'd react to her. That boy loved him some her.

She was adorable. She was so sweet to him. She knew how he felt about her, and she always took the time to run up to him and give him a big hug. That was when she could catch him. Normally he'd run just fast enough to make it look like he was retreating, but just slow enough that he'd get caught, and she'd pick him up and hug him. His flirt game was obviously well beyond his years.

It all started with a play date between her little sister and Cooper. She just happened to show up, and so did Macklin. He asked her if she would push him on the swing, and once she started, he never wanted her to stop. That was it. He was smitten. On the way home from the park that day, as he sat in his car seat staring out the window, he said, "Daddy, I really like that girl in the green shirt. She has beautiful lips."

He was just three-and-a-half at the time, and he was certain he'd found "the one." And from that moment on, he would take every opportunity he could to run into her. Mind you, he was in pre-school, so he really didn't have much to do with his schedule, but I did the best I could to make that happen for him. I knew that there was a really good chance that she'd slip away and meet someone her own age sooner than later, but one thing was for certain, Macklin wouldn't go down without a fight.

Valentine's Day was approaching, and Macklin wanted to do something special for this girl. Let's just call her Haiden. Because her name is Haiden. He told me that he'd really like to get her some red flowers and some candy but that he was really nervous about giving them to her. He explained to me that he doesn't know why he gets so nervous but that he just can't help it. And that anytime he sees her, his belly rumbles, and sometimes he even toots.

We talked back and forth about what we could do to help calm his nerves. I explained to him that if it was too much, we could take a rain check and give it a shot the following year. He replied that this was something that couldn't wait. That it was something that needed to happen. And that it needed to happen now. And then, seemingly out of nowhere, he figured it out. It wasn't me. I promise you that it wasn't me. It was all him. He told me he'd be right back, and he darted up to his room.

After a few minutes of anticipation, I heard the sound of his little footsteps coming down the stairs, and as he turned the corner, he said confidently,

"Daddy...

...I'll go as Batman!"

Yep. My dude figured it out. He was going to go deliver the gifts to probably the most popular girl at Cavett Elementary, in front of the entire school, on Valentine's Day, disguised as Batman.

I asked him how he had come to this decision; to him, it was quite simple. He claimed that if he dressed this way, she might know that it was him, but she might not. And he seemed to like that idea. He continued explaining that he would wear the mask just in case he got super nervous and turned red because she wouldn't be able to tell. And finally, he'd don the cape, just in case he needed to abort the mission and fly away

As we drove to school that next afternoon, I asked him if he was nervous, and he said, "not even a little." He waited patiently for her to appear. Dressed as Batman. In the snow. He didn't run away upon the sight of her. He stood his ground, and he stood it strong. He even disguised his voice to talk in a deeper Batman-like tone as he gave her the flowers and candy.

Cavett Elementary will never be the same. My dude ticked off a lot of 5th-grade boys that day. Probably not just the 5th-grade boys, but more than likely, most of the boys in the entire school. My dude became a legend that day. It was Valentine's Day 2019, and he did what others wouldn't dare do. He went for it.

I don't know about y'all, but in my life, I've been guilty of sitting around and waiting for perfect. I'll find myself waiting for the perfect moment. The perfect scenario. The perfect timing. The perfect everything. Sometimes I'll even find myself waiting for God to give me the perfect sign to go after the perfect situation at the perfect time. Knowing full well that that's not how life operates.

Maybe you're guilty of this too. Maybe you're looking at a career change. Maybe you'd like to travel more. Maybe you're wanting to start your own business. Maybe it's a new relationship you'd like to pursue or an old one you'd like to get out of. Or maybe it's a new hobby you're interested in.

But you just can't right now because you keep telling yourself:

My finances aren't in order.
I'm scared of change.

I'm too old.
I'm too young.
I'm worried it may not work.
I may not be any good at it.
I'm worried I might fail.
I've got way too much happening right now.
I'm just not sure.
Maybe next month.
Next year.
Next decade.

The scary thing is that we've been using these same excuses (or lies) for years now. These excuses have been ingrained in our heads so much that we've even started to believe them. This book is a perfect example. I kept telling myself:

"I'm too old to write the book. I'm worried no one will want to read it. I don't have the time to do it right now. There is just too much happening in my life. I don't even know where to start. How will I pay for it all? I'm just not sure. It'll probably fail anyway. Maybe next year. Or the following. Maybe."

Guys, I consider myself a really positive, encouraging, uplifting person. And I hate to be the one that has to break this to you, but it's time. Someone needs to tell you. Are you ready for it?

Ok, here we go. Perfect isn't coming. It doesn't just show up at your door with a big ol' sign announcing that it's arrived. I wish that were the case, but life doesn't work that way.

Macklin's "Batman moment" was the farthest thing from perfect. All the odds were stacked against him. The haters would have given him no shot. Heck, even his biggest supporters would have doubted his decision. They would have told him that he was too young. Too short. Not strong enough. Not fast enough. Not bold enough. That this was far from the perfect situation. That there was a great chance that she would ignore him and that he was setting himself up for complete embarrassment and failure.

But that's not what happened. Because he went for it. Because he did it. And at that moment, he proved to all of us that on the other side of the imperfections, distractions, doubters, excuses, and lies, something is waiting. And it may just be as close to perfect as it gets.

JUST DO! CHALLENGE:

How long have you been waiting for that perfect situation to go for something? What is that one thing you would love to do (and you know that you should do) but are holding back because the timing or scenario just isn't perfect? If you're waiting for a sign, here it is. Here is your invitation to just go for it. It's never going to be perfect. There will be some big ol' hurdles and probably a bunch of them. But it's always worth it on the other side. The lesson here isn't to dress up in a Batman costume and go after something you're too nervous to pursue. The lesson is to just do and if it happens to take a Batman costume to do it, then go get yourself one. And go as Batman.

LESSON 12:
"DID YOU ASK JESUS TO FIX IT?"

"Hey buddy, I can't play right now," I said as Macklin begged me to get off the couch and play something, anything, with him.

"Why not, Daddy?," he questioned.

"Buddy, my belly hurts really bad, and I just need to lay here for a while," I responded.

"Did you ask Jesus to fix it?," he asked. "Don't worry, daddy, I'll ask Him to fix it," he said as he bowed his head and began to pray.

That conversation with Macklin completely changed my entire world when it came to spending time with Jesus. It was just a little stomachache, probably self-induced, from the wings I had eaten earlier that day and/or the fact that I'd skipped the gym that morning.

Of course, I didn't ask Jesus to fix it. I only ask Jesus to fix the big things in my life. Not the little things. This just wasn't a big enough thing to talk to Him about. Looking back, at that moment, the really big thing for Macklin was that I get up and play with him. For him, it was absolutely prayer worthy. And at the same time, he was so confused why I hadn't thought to ask Jesus to fix it.

I don't know about y'all, but I tend to just take my bigger battles to Jesus. Yes, I pray for my meals, but if I'm being honest, it's short and sweet and more of a habit than anything. Yes, I pray before bedtime. But those prayers are a lot like my meal prayers. They aren't quite the "now I lay me down to sleep" kind of prayers, but close enough. And yes, in high school, I absolutely prayed that if He'd only give me the girl or if He'd just help us win that basketball game, I'd never ask for a thing again. Until I did.

It's easy to take our big battles to Jesus and forget how much He cares about all the little stuff too. I don't know about you, but I didn't give thanks when my car started this morning. I didn't give thanks for the hot water I had in my shower last night. I didn't say thanks for a good night's sleep or for the fact that I didn't get in a car accident on my way to Starbucks this morning.

Imagine this: It's your perfect day. The weather is fabulous. You're with the people you love the most, doing the things you love the most. Maybe that's a lake day, maybe you're on the golf course, or maybe you're up in the mountains. But wherever you are, you are exactly where you want to be, and you couldn't be any happier. Then, all of a sudden, you get a text with some really incredible news. This is something you've been praying about for quite some time. You've been working so hard for it, and it's finally happening. You hit your knees and praise God for hearing your prayers and making this plan come together.

I'd have done the exact same thing. I'd have been so happy and praising the Lord for all His blessings. But let's backtrack for a minute. Do you remember the perfect day, with the ideal weather, with the people you love so much? Who do you think orchestrated that? Did you thank God for those moments too? For what it's worth, I forgot. But man, He's working in those moments too.

I'm not here to preach. That's not what I do. But I do think it's important to be reminded, even if it takes a four-year-old that just wants to play catch, that God can work in all things, not just the big, momentous things.

Yes, He's a miracle worker, way-maker, deliverer, all-powerful, and mighty God. But sometimes it's easy to forget that He's also a God of really beautiful days. A God that cares deeply about the people He brings into our lives. A God of all the tiny details and moments that don't seem so big at the time. I don't know about you, but in my life, He has a history of using what seems like insignificant things and molding them into monumental changes in my life.

I mentioned earlier that a new business opportunity was what brought our family to Nebraska. What I didn't mention is why we were even looking for an opportunity. The company that I'd been a part of, the one that gave us the means to live the RV life, and the one that opened up so many doors for our family, had begun a rapid decline. Our monthly income went from a whole bunch to very little. And it happened seemingly overnight. I'd never been at this point in my life, but it got so bad for a little while that I remember waking up each morning and not having any idea how we'd do dinner that night.

I know what you're thinking. "You never mentioned any of this on Instagram." You're right. People don't want to see the messy stuff over there, and I sure didn't want people to think we were struggling. I had a reputation to uphold and having $12 in my bank account wasn't something I was proud of or wanted to tell the world. So I didn't. I kept it to myself. Until now.

I was so mad at God. I couldn't believe He would allow this thing that I'd worked so hard for over the past five years to come crashing down. I didn't understand what He was doing. Or why He was doing it. It made no sense in the world to me. What did I do to deserve this? Why would He cause me so much stress and pain and uncertainty? Why God? Why?

What I couldn't see and what was beyond my understanding at the time was the season that He was preparing me for. At the time, it was so unclear to me. At the time, I was so angry. At the time, I doubted what God was doing. At the time, I saw no goodness in any of this. And at the time, I was blind to the fact that He was working wonders behind the scenes of our messy lives to make sure we were ready for what was to come.

Fast forward eight months, and it all made sense. It was all so clear.

Rachel and I sat at the edge of our bed in silence. I'm not even sure how long we sat there. Maybe it was seconds, maybe minutes, maybe an hour. I just remember how quiet it was. We had just hung up the phone with our oncologist, confirming exactly what we'd suspected. It was, in fact, cancer.

Rachel eventually broke the silence.

"Ok, now we know. And now we go beat this. That's what we are going to do."

I know you're probably thinking, wait, why was it all clear now? How does getting cancer make this all make sense? Well, I'm glad you asked. There are a million little reasons. I don't have the time or the space in this book to list them all, but when I tell you there were a million little things, I mean it and here are just a few:

1. Let's start with Lincoln, Nebraska. I didn't want to go there. I couldn't figure out why this was our next stop. It was way too cold, and there was nothing for me there. Until we got that call. And it turns out that of all the places in the world, Lincoln would be the perfect place to fight cancer. Once we found out what we were dealing with, we searched high and low to ensure we had the best doctors in the world. And believe it or not, those doctors were right there in Lincoln. We were right where we needed to be. Only God can orchestrate such a thing.

2. Rachel's parents lived in Kansas City, which happens to be only a few hours away from Lincoln. Not to mention, a year prior, Rachel's dad retired. This allowed them to be at our place at any given moment. And it turned out there would be a whole lot of "given" moments. God knew this was where we needed to be, and He knew how much we'd need them around. Only God can orchestrate such a thing.

3. Nannies. We spent a lot of time at different doctors for chemo, radiation, and checkups. And when we weren't at the doctor, I had to work, and Rachel had to rest. At the same time, we had three kids that needed to eat and go to school and be taken care of. God knew this, so he sent a couple of angels disguised as nannies into our family's life. With cancer comes a ton of uncertainty, and you aren't really sure what the next day will bring. If it wasn't for our nannies, Hannah and Alexa, showing up and loving us so well, right where we were, I'm not sure how we would have done it. Only God can orchestrate such a thing.

4. Insurance. You don't think a ton about it until you need it. And we had no idea how badly we'd need it. Yes, we had insurance previously, but I was an independent contractor, and our insurance was terrible. It took my company sinking and my income becoming non-existent for me to realize I needed to find something else. It made zero sense to me at the time but had that not happened, there's an excellent chance we would be staring at mountains of medical debt for the rest of our lives. Only He can orchestrate such a thing.

5. Community. I talked about this earlier when I mentioned all the things I hated about Lincoln. But if you remember right, the thing that I loved most was its people. The people at our church. The people at our kids' schools. The people that Rachel knew from her past time there. The people that loved on us, surrounded us, prayed for us, and cared for us. The people that showed up and expected nothing in return. The people that didn't ask what they could do for us. The people that just did. Only God can orchestrate such a thing.

When everything was going bad. When my company was crashing. When I didn't have enough money to pay for a tank of gas. When I had no idea how we'd be able to pay the bills to make it to the end of the month. When I wasn't sure how to tell Rachel that we were officially broke. God was faithful. The entire time. He was working. The entire time. He was there. The entire time.

You see, I was praying. I was asking God to fix it. And though I couldn't see it at the time because it wasn't the fix I was asking for, He was fixing it. He was fixing it much better than I could have ever imagined. That's what He does. He's a fixer. He fixes things. The biggest of big things. The smallest of small things. And everything in between. Even a self-induced bellyache.

JUST DO! CHALLENGE:

Do you ever question what God's doing in your life? Yeah, me too. Do you have doubts about what He's up to? I feel ya. Are you confused and having trouble seeing the good? I'm with you. Or maybe for you, everything is good, and it's almost like you're coasting through this season of life. Maybe the biggest hindrance in your day is a bellyache. If that's the case, I want to challenge you to take a second and thank Him for that. And then ask Him to fix your bellyache so you can go play.

On the other hand, maybe things seem to be falling apart all around you, and you can't figure out why He would allow this to happen. You're not alone. I've been there. We've all been there. And I just want to encourage you that He's up to something. He's up to something bigger than you can even begin to comprehend. It may not be clear to you tomorrow or next week, or even next month, but I can promise you, one day, it will be. One day you'll be thanking Him for the hard times that you're enduring now because of what He's building for you in the future. And you may even find yourself thanking Him for not giving you the girl you prayed so hard for.

THE "C" WORD

"WHY NOT US?"

April 17, 2018

That day used to have zero significance in my life. And now, each year when it rolls around, it stings a little bit. April 17, 2018, was the day we got the news. That was the day we sat quietly, for who knows how long, staring at each other at the end of our bed, trying to comprehend what it all meant. It didn't seem real. I mean, Rachel was too young. She was too healthy. She had done everything right. She didn't deserve to have cancer. No one deserves to have cancer. But she SURE didn't deserve to have it. And how do we tell the kids? How do we tell our parents? How do we tell our friends? And what about everyone else? Do we even tell everyone else?

Rachel and I went back and forth on this idea. On the one hand, we didn't want to share the cancer news with the masses because we knew that everyone was going through their own "hard," and we never wanted anyone to think that we felt ours was harder or deserved more attention. On the other hand, we wanted to let people know what we were going through, not for sympathy but for prayers and awareness.

So after we told our kids that mommy had "booby cancer," and we told our families and close friends the news, we decided we did indeed want to tell everyone else. And this is what that looked like from our Facebook post on April 24th:

> *Usually, when people post things on Facebook, they're announcing something good to the world. Things like "We're engaged!" Or, "We're pregnant!" Or, "We purchased our first home!!" Or, "It's a boy!" Or, "I got*

the job!!" Or, "Our town just got a Chick-fil-A!" Or something fun like that.

And for those who know Rachel and me, you know that we tend to keep things pretty positive. We don't really do negativity in our lives. Life is way too short, and we are way too blessed to pay attention to things that aren't awesome. And I so wish more than anything that this was going to be an "Our town just got a Chick-fil-A" post.

But it's not.

So what do you do when something sucky slaps you in the face, and you're not sure what to do about it? You can't just disappear. You can't just avoid it in hopes it goes away. We honestly don't know what the right thing to do is. But this is our way. We've gone back and forth with this decision on whether or not to share this publicly, and in the end, we want people to know because we want people to pray. That's it. We aren't looking for anything else but prayers! We so believe in the power of prayer, and we know we have so many amazing people in our lives that will actually pray with us. Not just say, "praying for you" or "prayers going up" or "🙏" But actually pray.

I promise that this post isn't for sympathy. And honestly, please do me a favor and don't text or call Rachel because responding to people about your cancer diagnosis ain't fun. Honestly, how do you respond? We don't know how to respond yet. It's hard to respond because we just don't know how to. Other than thanks, and we appreciate it. It's hard. We aren't good at this quite yet. She knows y'all care. She knows y'all love her. She knows we have the best support system in the world. And we so appreciate that. But the reason we are making this post is to simply *ask if you would pray with us. If you would just please pray.*

So last week, Rachel was diagnosed with breast cancer. And to be honest, it sucked. It rocked our world. We were in complete shock. You just don't expect that to happen. Not to us. So many thoughts. So many worries. So much anxiety. Lots of waiting and praying and waiting and praying. And, of course, wondering how to tell our families, our friends, and the kids. I mean, how do you tell your kids that mommy is sick? Mommies aren't supposed to be sick. They aren't just mommies...they are superheroes. They do it all. How do you explain to your kids that mommy is going to be going to the doctor a whole lot? That she may be too tired to go to your dance class or your school play? That she's gonna take lots of naps and may not be at dinner every night? That she may lose some weight and will probably even lose her hair? How do you tell them that they may have a bald mommy?

So, for now, we are just taking it a day at a time. And we understand that this is our hard right now.

After the initial shock and thoughts of "Why us? Why would God make us go through this? What did we do to deserve this?" We quickly shifted those thoughts and conversations to "why not us?" Why should it be anyone but us? We trust God with all that we are. We know that He loves us like no one else can. So why not choose us? I mean, we have the most incredible people surrounding us, we serve an awesome God, and He chose us to fight this battle. I don't know why this is happening right now, but why <u>not</u> us?

I think it's easy to have that outlook knowing I have a spunky, stubborn, bad-to-the-bone wife in Rachel. We all know that she doesn't take crap from anyone. She calls it like it is, and she's a fighter. Rachel always has been and will continue to be the rock of this family. Together we will fight the heck out of this, and we will beat it. That's what we are going to do.

Guys, we are blessed. Blessed with amazing family, friends, and co-workers who have been willing to bend over backward to make sure we are ok. We are at peace with this diagnosis. We have no idea what this is going to look like. This is new to us. We don't know what the road ahead will have in store. The initial reports haven't been perfect. They call it an "aggressive cancer." I'm not even sure what that means but what this cancer doesn't know quite yet is that I've got an aggressive wife, and we have an aggressive support system, and we plan to "agress" the heck out of this stupid cancer.

So, where are we right now? Yesterday she got a port put in because they want us to start chemo pretty quickly. As in this Friday. The major fear of the aggression was that this stuff had spread everywhere. But we got some great news today from the oncologist... IT HASN'T SPREAD! It's pretty contained in her breast and lymph nodes. So see, things are already looking up! I mean, who knew a great day would be when you find out it's just breast cancer?!

Here is the deal. We know that everyone has something going on in their personal lives, and there's no way to begin to prioritize what's a bigger something than the next. Everyone is battling something. Everyone has a "hard" in their lives. This just happens to be our something right now. This is our hard. And all we can say is that we love y'all for loving us so hard during our hard!

Honestly, my hope is that by making this 'Facebook Official,' we will have so many people praying for Rachel and the kids that all those in heaven will know something big is happening down here. They will know that Rachel is so loved that they may even get a little jealous because they've never seen so many prayers for one person before. That's my hope. That's why we are going public.

We hadn't told many people until today, but we've been overwhelmed by the support we've been given by those closest to us. Thank you doesn't say enough. I know some of you may be a bit upset that we didn't call you or tell you sooner and that you had to find out this way... But do you know what one of the least fun things to do on earth is? After being told you or your spouse has cancer. It's to sit down and call all of your friends and loved ones, one at a time, to tell them that you or your spouse has cancer. It's not fun. It's uncomfortable for you and for us. What do you say? How are you supposed to react? I guess you don't quite grasp it till it hits home but sharing a cancer diagnosis is super messy. It's ugly. It's scary. It sucks. But it's necessary. You can't hide this. And there isn't an easy or right way to go about telling all those people that you love. So this was our way. Today you got our way. And this is the best we have to give.

Oh, and a little advice for everyone out there - If you ever need a little reminder of just how loved you are, get cancer. Or I got an even better idea; just take my word for it. We are loved, and you are too.

Here is what I know. She will fight. She will win. We will fight. We will win. This will be a battle. Probably a really long one. But we are ready. We are ready for our something. We are ready for our hard. And of all the people that could have had this happen to them, we say, "Why not us?"

So that's how we told the world. Well, not the world, but that's how we told Facebook. Which at that time was the only way we knew how to tell our world. And more importantly, it was the best way for us to ask that anyone in the world that would be willing to pray for us to do just that. And it worked. It worked so big. I remember feeling overwhelmed by all the love we received from so many people. I mean, there was no doubt that heaven was feeling the prayers. We not only had loved ones praying for us, but we had people that we didn't even know and people I didn't even think liked us praying for us. Heck, we even have people that said they had never prayed before, praying for us.

It really is wild how life comes at you. It is an incredible adventure. The fact is - one moment, things in your life can be going amazingly perfect. And then, seemingly out of nowhere, life slaps you in the face. And then, all of a sudden, it's amazing again. And in between the amazing and the slaps in the face, there lies a bunch of "ordinary" sprinkled in there somewhere. I encourage you to take in the amazing, to embrace the face slaps, and to love the ordinary.

We could have responded in many different ways to this diagnosis. Anger, sadness, regret, self-pity; just to name a few. But instead, I got to be a witness to something extraordinary. I had a front-row seat to watch how Rachel responded and what she chose. I'm not even sure you'll believe me when I tell you this. Out of all the emotions that she could have chosen when this terrible diagnosis came our way...she chose joy.

Joy is a decision, a really brave one, about how you are going to respond to life.

Rachel responded perfectly.

Rachel chose joy.

BOOB GUY VS. BUTT GUY

They say there are two types of guys in this world. Boob guys and butt guys. If you would have asked me where I stood on this topic prior to Rachel's diagnosis, I think I would have leaned towards the boob side. But then, in 2018, Rachel's boobs tried to kill her. Once that happened, I decided I was no longer a fan of boobs. To me, they are the worst. I'd been transformed.

Around our house, 2018 had become known as the "year of cancer." Because when you have cancer, it becomes an all-consuming thing in your life. 2018 wasn't my favorite year to date. Not even close. Nothing about cancer is fun. The 36 rounds of radiation weren't fun. The eight rounds of chemo weren't fun. The total hysterectomy, again, not fun. Watching Rachel be sick for most of the year wasn't fun. The kids having to watch their mommy hurt so much wasn't fun. Me having to watch the kids watch their mommy hurt so much wasn't fun. I think you get the point. The entire year, and all that came with cancer, wasn't very much fun.

But the great news, on the other side of all the "fun" that 2018 brought into our lives was that we beat it. I say "we" because cancer doesn't just come for the patient. It comes for the entire tribe. But what mattered most was that we beat it. The chemo worked. The radiation worked. The doctors were thrilled with where we were. And we were so happy to finally put 2018 behind us and we couldn't wait to see what 2019 had in store for us.

But before we could close the book on the year of cancer, there was one more thing that we had to do. The kids called it "booby removal day," but I think the medical term is a double mastectomy. If you followed our story, we were very open about everything with our kids. We decided early on that because we had no idea how long the cancer journey would be, the last thing we wanted to do was whisper or hide things from our kids. Because the truth was, we were all in this together. So even when it came to booby removal day, it was no different. We were in this together, and the kids all had very different reactions to what was about to go down.

Hadley was worried sick. She hadn't shown much emotion until the night before the surgery. She was just really scared. She didn't care one bit about what happened to mommy's boobies, as long as mommy was ok.

Cooper was really confused and just wanted mommy to have her hair back. And she also thought it was funny that when the surgery was over, her boobies would be the same size as her mommy's.

Macklin said he was gonna miss mommy's "big boobs" and wanted his mommy to have "ginormous boobies" one day soon. (See above, it's pretty apparent that Macklin is a boob guy.)

You see, cancer picked the wrong family to mess with. The point is, if you mess with someone we love, whether it's a family member, a friend, our neighbors, or anyone we care about, we'll just remove you. Ok, maybe we won't remove you. But in the case of Rachel's boobs, they messed with us, and they were goners.

Even though 2018 was a hard and stupid year, we learned some pretty great lessons along the way. We learned that most things in life take a back seat to cancer. We learned that the results of a college football game really don't matter that much in the grand scheme of things. Really, we learned that *most things* really don't matter that much in the grand scheme of things. We learned to worry a lot less about the stupid stuff and that most of the stuff that we worry about is stupid stuff. I learned that you don't know when you marry a woman what she'll look like bald until she's bald. Rachel had the cutest bald head you'd ever seen.

And most of all, we learned that God is so good, and we were reminded once again that people are so kind.

It wasn't difficult at all for us to say goodbye to 2018. To cancer. To treatments. To all the things that came at us that year. We were thrilled to finally put it all behind us and to move on. For us, moving on was more than just saying goodbye to 2018; it also meant saying goodbye to Nebraska.

We spent 22 months in Lincoln. We knew when we got there that it wouldn't be permanent. In 22 months, we saw 19 months of winter. Winter came. Winter stayed. When we arrived, I was pretty much ready to leave. You see, my goal was to do my best not to get close to anyone while I was there. I told Rachel that we weren't there to stay and that I didn't want to find people to love only to have to leave them. But those dang people made it really hard to live that way. Yes, they had some crazy tendencies and ate some weird stuff. But they were impossible not to love, no matter how hard I tried not to love them.

Nebraska's state motto is "The Good Life," and for a while, I was so confused about what they were thinking or drinking when they came up with this. But after 22 months, I got it. I knew that I was gonna miss that place. I knew that I was gonna miss those people. And though we were so excited to move back to Knoxville and leave the cancer chapter behind us, I knew that I was gonna miss, "The Good Life."

WITH YOU

This chapter will be short. Heck, it may not even be considered a chapter but I didn't know what else to call it. So a chapter it is. I just know that it's important, so please don't skip it.

For those of you that know our story, you know what's coming next. You know that we were in remission for a very short time. You know that in 2019 the cancer came back. And you probably even know where we are today. But before we get into all of that, I want to take a moment to encourage those that are going through a cancer scare right now. And those that may have one coming their way.

Listen, I don't know much but I know that most people beat this stupid disease. I don't want you to see the outcome of our story and immediately think that things will end the way for you that they did for us. That's not how this usually works. Cancer is not a death sentence. Every 30 seconds someone gets diagnosed with cancer. And one in two of us will get diagnosed with some sort of cancer in our lifetimes. But guess what, one in two of us won't die because of it. Not even close.

I just want you to know that there is a better than excellent chance you're going to be ok! I believe in you. I believe in your story. And I believe that you have a lot more story to tell. And until there is a reason to believe any differently, that's what I choose to believe. I hope you'll believe that with me. Please believe that with me.

You are so loved and you're not alone.

I'm with you.

I HATE GOOGLE

"**B**aby, my back hurts really bad, and I think the cancer is back," Rachel said to me one morning as casually as she'd ask for her morning coffee.

"Wait, what? Why would you even say such a stupid thing?" I replied.

I chalked it up to getting old. My back hurts a lot as well. That's what happens when you turn 40. Back pain. Neck pain. Shoulder pain. Foot pain. Pain in places you didn't know pain could even happen.

Rachel explained to me that this was different. That Google had told her what it was and that it wasn't good. She had spent the entire night Googling different things, and she knew exactly what was going on. The cancer had come back, and it was now in her spine, and it wasn't going away this time.

I never wanted her to be wrong so badly in my entire life. But as she always seemed to be, she was right. So on August 16, 2019, we went to Facebook and had to do something I never expected to have to do again. Until I did.

Well...this sucks. And we certainly didn't have it in our plans to make a post like this in 2019. We had to do it in 2018, and it sucked then, and we'd thought we had crossed that type of post off our bucket list.

But we find ourselves here again coming to y'all not to announce a move (btw, for those that missed it, we did move to Tennessee), not to announce a new job (btw, for those that missed it, Rachel did get a new job), not to announce a pregnancy (btw, for those that missed it, we are officially done having children), but to announce that the dang cancer has come back.

I know, I know, Rachel just got done beating it. I know, I know, it just doesn't make sense. I know, I know, I didn't think it could come back this quick, either. I know, I know, this really sucks.

Long story short, for the past few weeks, Rachel has been in a lot of pain. After a few MRIs, some CT scans, a lumbar puncture, a biopsy, a visit with the radiation oncologist, and a bunch of other appointments where doctors used a lot of big words that I didn't quite understand, we learned that Rachel's cancer has now metastasized and that it has gotten into her bones.

If you Google what that means, it's kinda scary. So I'd just advise you to stay away from Google. I'll tell you what, watch this. I'll be your Google:

Hey Google, "What does Metastatic Breast Cancer mean?"
   - About 21,600,000 results (0.75 seconds)
   - Metastatic Breast Cancer: It's stupid. It sucks. It's scary. It will probably hurt. It will be super annoying, and it might not ever go away. It's just really, really, really stupid.

See, I told you it's not fun to Google it. But I knew you probably would anyway, so I did it for you. You're welcome.

Needless to say, we've got a long road ahead. A battle. Probably a war. For sure harder than the last time. And this time, it's not really going away, so it's something that we will live with for the rest of our lives. It's scarier. It's uglier. It's suckier.

But it's hard for me to believe that the end result will be any different. We will fight the fight. We will punch back harder than ever before. And I'm certain we will win this round and any other round that comes our way.

See, cancer is stupid. And all too often, it picks on the wrong people. The wrong families. The wrong tribes.

With all the people that we have surrounding us…
With all the prayer warriors praying with us…
With all of our incredible family and all of our amazing friends…
With the Awesome God that we serve…
…it's impossible to believe the outcome will be any different this time.
Cancer chose the wrong person yet again. You'd think it would have learned from the last time, but as I said, cancer is stupid.

Rachel is literally the strongest human being on the planet. She's kind of a superhero around these parts. Wait, actually, this just in, and it's confirmed; she's a superhero around all parts. She will fight this, and she will fight it with so much grace and class that it's almost impossible to understand from the outside looking in.

So here is the deal… We still don't know exactly what this round will look like. We don't necessarily know all of our treatment options yet. There is still so much to learn and understand. But we do know there will be a bunch more doctor appointments in our future. We know that our family is going to do this all over again. We know we are ready for whatever comes our way. And if you've met our kids, you know that they are ready to fight this thing right along with us. They, too, are superheroes as far as I'm concerned.

And just like last time, we want to invite you to fight with us. Just like last time, the thing that we need more than anything is your prayers. That's it. We so believe in the power of prayer, and we simply can't have enough. The last time y'all showed up, y'all showed up so big, y'all prayed hard, y'all prayed often, and cancer didn't stand a chance. So if y'all would be willing to do that once again, I promise I won't ever ask for anything from y'all again.

I know to many of y'all, this doesn't make any sense, and it's easy to wonder why this is happening again. Believe me; I get it. I feel that way all too often. But in the end, I always come back to this - as hard as this is to understand, I know that we serve a God who allows hurt and who also allows pain. But I also know we serve a God who uses hurt and pain for good. So, friends, we can all take heart in knowing that our pain, our hurt, and our tears will not be wasted.

We love y'all. We appreciate y'all. And we are so grateful that so many of y'all will fight this right by our side. Now let's go kick cancer's butt once again.

And once again, people showed up. People showed up so big. The way people showed up was a testament to how Rachel lived her life. To the way that she cared for others. To the way that she loved people so well. She didn't spend her life doing that just in case something like this ever happened to her. She spent her life doing that because that's what we are supposed to do. She just lived it better than most.

I was so inspired by the amount of love that came our way that I wrote, what I thought, was a seemingly insignificant blog that a few friends may read. What I thought would happen was wrong. What actually happened was incredible. Here's that blog...

Wanna Feel Loved? Get Cancer.

The cancer was supposed to be gone. We'd already beaten it once. We had even taken a celebration trip with our friends and family to Palm Springs and toasted the fact that the final results had come in and that we had kicked cancer's butt.

But it came back. And it wasn't supposed to come back. At least, I didn't think it was supposed to come back. And it for sure wasn't supposed to come back this fast. I mean, we beat it. It was gone. We had our "cancer chapter," and we sure didn't need to have another one.

But you see, cancer doesn't care what you want or what you feel, or what you think is fair. Cancer is a bitch. I'm sorry I cussed, but there just isn't another word for it. Cancer is a "B." It can ruin plans, it can ruin finances, it can ruin relationships, and it can even ruin lives. It doesn't care how much or how little money you have. It doesn't care if you're educated or not. It doesn't care what religion you are or what you believe. I'm just letting you know that cancer doesn't care what your agenda is because it has its own.

When the cancer came back, Hadley was eight, Cooper was seven, and Macklin was five. We never hid Mommy's cancer from them. We were honest. We were open. We cried together. We laughed together. We enjoyed the good days Mommy had, and we even embraced the hard days. We realized that we really didn't have a choice in the matter. So we just embraced all the days, because some days, having another day is all we could ask for.

You see, a few years ago, we didn't live like that. We took days, weeks, and even years for granted. We lived our lives like we had an unlimited amount of time left. We don't do that anymore. We don't take a single moment for granted. We can't afford to. And if you get nothing out of reading this, get that. Because you can't afford to, either. You just don't know what tomorrow holds. So, love your people and love them hard. Don't wait for a diagnosis or a tragedy or death to do this. Please. Just trust me on this one.

And if we're being completely honest (and I am because no one can tell me not to be right now), in the end, everyone has their "hard." Our hard just happened to be cancer in that season. But each and every one of us is dealing with (or will be dealing with) hard, sooner than later.

Maybe you are on the chopping block at work, and you know layoffs are on the way. Losing a job is super hard.

Maybe you and your spouse have tried for years and years and just can't get pregnant. Infertility is super hard.

Maybe you've got a family member or a friend that struggles with addiction and can't seem to kick the habit no matter how many times an overdose causes death to knock at their door. Addiction is super hard.

Maybe you and your spouse fight nonstop, and you both know where this is heading. Divorce is super hard.

Maybe every day is a struggle for you and just getting out of bed each morning is your biggest victory. Depression is super hard.

Everyone has their hard. And unfortunately, we live in a society where all too often, we ignore other people's hards. I'm not saying that was the case with us. Trust me, that was far from the case. I mean it when I say, "Wanna feel loved? Get cancer." Because never in our lives had we felt so loved and cared for.

But that may not be the case for the barista you ignore each morning who heads home after each shift only to take care of her dying mother.

Or the flight attendant you lost your patience with last week who is going through a messy divorce, can't seem to get her life together, and has been contemplating suicide each night in every new city she's in.

Or the coworker who gets on your nerves so much you simply ignore her day in and day out. Did you know she leaves work only to head home to her abusive spouse?

Or the single mom you just had to flip off when she accidentally cut you off today on the way to work. Did you know her son was just deployed overseas for the first time last night?

Or maybe it was me. Maybe you were the one that sat next to me on the plane on that red eye I took from LA to Knoxville the evening it was confirmed that the cancer had in fact spread to Rachel's brain. You didn't know that, barring a miracle, my wife's cancer wasn't going to go away. And that the survival odds of someone with this type of cancer weren't in our favor. You didn't know that we had tens of thousands of dollars in medical bills that continued to stack up each day because some of these specialists didn't take our insurance. And that, to be honest, we didn't really care how much debt we accrued because nothing else mattered except getting her better. You didn't have to experience the roller coaster of emotions when a week prior, we were told by one doctor we had brain cancer and 24 hours later, another doctor told us we didn't. So at that point we didn't know what to know. Now we know. But, you didn't know.

Of course you didn't know.

But I was that guy. The guy next to you. And as you complained about there not being enough ice in your drink and about the baby that wouldn't stop crying in the back of the plane, my wife was at home with a pounding headache that hadn't gone away for three straight weeks because it turns out that she had tumors spreading all throughout her brain. And that at that moment, when you were annoyed with your lack of ice, I was pondering whether or not my kids would have their mommy this Christmas or not.

You weren't supposed to know that. And I didn't tell you any of that. I wouldn't want to put that on you.

The point is that we just don't know who we will come across today and what they are going through. We have no idea what their hard is, but there is a really good chance it's there. And we need to be better. I'm not saying we need to be better at recognizing their hards because, more often than not, it won't be evident.

But we need to understand that people are hurting all around us, and we need to be better. We need to be more kind. We need to have more patience. We need to give more grace. We need to love people more.

And finally, when you do know that someone is going through a hard, spend less time asking what you can do for them and just do.

There wasn't a day that went by during our cancer season where I wasn't asked by those that love us, "What can I do to help?" And I absolutely loved that so many wanted to help. It truly was (and still is) incredible how much people wanted to help. But in the end, even I didn't know what I could do to help make this better. I couldn't fix this, and that was so hard for me. Most days, I couldn't do a thing to make it better, and most days, you wouldn't have been able to, either. So when people would ask me what they could do, I had no idea how to respond because I just didn't know. Looking back on it now, I'd just encourage you that instead of asking what you can do for anyone going through a hard - just do.

If you want to take them a meal, do it. If you want to send a gift card or a note, do it. If you want to pray for them, do it. If you want to hug them, just hug them and hug them hard. Don't ask for permission, just do. Whatever that thing is that you want to do, just do. That's one of the most beautiful things about love. It just does.

But I must warn you. Do with no expectations of anything in return. Don't do this for you; do this for them. Because in the end, this isn't about you. This is all about them. You may not get a thank you, not because they aren't grateful, but because they have lost the capacity to even remember who has done what for them. You may show up and not be able to see them, not because they don't want to see you, but because for the first time in three days, the headache has gone away, and they can actually rest. Just do, with zero expectations at all. Just do, because that's what we are supposed to do, and that's how love is supposed to look.

"SO, MOMMY WILL BE BETTER ON FRIDAY?"

We were blown away by the reaction to that little blog. Millions of views and shares. A ton of invites to appear on different news channels and podcasts. Rachel even joked with me during one of our many doctors' appointments, "Babe, you're welcome for getting cancer, so you could go viral."

As cute as that was for her to say, we both knew that viral was never the goal. Gaining followers or views didn't matter a bit. But awareness and prayers had always been the goal. So if a few of those million readers were now praying for us, we hit our goal. We actually turned down most requests to appear on anything because Rachel rarely felt up to it, or we were in the middle of another appointment. We were just trying to find a plan that helped. We were trying to stay positive. And full transparency, we were just trying to live another day.

It was the night before Rachel and I were heading off to MD Anderson to meet with some new doctors who had developed a new treatment plan they thought would be our best shot at living more days. For those that aren't familiar, MD Anderson is one of the top cancer hospitals in the world. And at this point, we needed the best in the world.

As I lay down on the floor next to Hadley's bed after saying our prayers, I told her that I had some good news and some bad news. The bad news was that Mommy and Daddy had to go to Houston for about a week. But the good news was that we were going to get to meet the most amazing doctors in the world, and they were going to do all that they could to help mommy get better.

She responded, "Ok, well, I'm sad that you and mommy will be gone for a week and that you'll miss my soccer game, but I'm mostly happy because you get to meet the best doctors in the world to help mommy get better."

"Me too, Sweetie. Me too," I said.

After a few minutes of silence, I assumed she was asleep, so I started to get up to leave her room, when Hadley curiously asked, "So, how does it happen so fast, Daddy?"

"How does what happen so fast?" I replied.

"You said that you were meeting with the doctors that will help mommy get better," she answered. "That's fast that Mommy will be better on Friday."

Imagine for a moment having to explain to your eight-year-old that that's not exactly how it works. In those few minutes of silence, she had talked herself into the fact that her mommy was going to be better when we got back on Friday, which wasn't actually true. Imagine the bedtime conversations that took place that year. Better yet, don't. You don't need to do that. I'll keep some of those to myself. No parent should have to have those conversations.

Watching Rachel be sick was really hard. But there were many moments when watching the kids watch their mommy be sick may have even been harder.

I explained to Hadley that mommy wouldn't come back all better but that we would come back with a plan that could help her get better. And that's exactly what we did.

We had a new plan. And that plan gave us hope. That was the word that we used as we left MD Anderson that week. We were hopeful. And considering some of the feelings that we'd had lately, hopeful was a nice change of pace. There were still a ton of unknowns, but leaving with a new plan seemed better than what we had arrived with.

We had hope that Rachel would get better. We were told that we may not see immediate results, but we did start seeing some encouraging signs pretty quickly. Her back pain got a little better. She was getting out of bed more frequently. She was on her feet more often. She was still dizzy most of the time and super nauseous all of the time, but it had only been a week or so. And just the fact that anything good was happening, no matter how small, was super encouraging to all of us. We took all the good that we could find, and we were grateful for it.

Maybe she was turning the corner.

Maybe she was getting better.

Maybe not as soon as Friday.

But maybe soon.

And at that point, "maybe" was enough.

THE PINK RIBBON

Confession: For the first 36 years of my life, I didn't know that October was Breast Cancer Awareness Month. And I'm really sorry for that. I think it's selfish that I didn't know that. There are so many of you that have been affected by this terrible disease, and I'm sorry that it had to hit so close to home for me to see it. Breast cancer is the most common cancer in women and the fact that about 1 in 8 women will get it during their lifetime makes me sick.

I would see the pink ribbon here and there; on someone's license plate or a t-shirt or a golf ball. But before we got it, it never meant much to me. And I'm so sorry. I'm embarrassed by that. I just need you to know that I get it now. That I see it now. And that I'm in your corner.

If you've gone through it, I'm sorry I wasn't there for you when you were in the throes of it.

If you're going through it now, I promise you that I'm here to go through it with you.

And for those of you who may be heading into it, I'm not going anywhere. And I'll be there when and if you need someone. Someone to cry with. To laugh with. To cuss with. To drink with. To pray with. I'll be there.

One of the most difficult parts of our cancer journey for me was that I couldn't fix it. I am a fixer, and there was nothing I could do to fix this. And at the same time, as much as I wanted to, I could never truly relate to what Rachel was going through. I could watch the pain she was in, and even though it hurt me so much, it wasn't my pain. I could be there by her side at every appointment, but it was never my body that they were scanning.

I could sit with her in the chemo room each time we had to go, but it was never my arm they put a needle into.

I was there. I was always there. But to say that I could relate to what she was going through just wouldn't be true. And today, if you're personally battling cancer, any kind of cancer, I'd be lying if I said that I could relate to you. Because I just can't. And I'm sorry.

But to the person who is driving you to and from each appointment, I can relate. To the one who is holding your hand while you get treatment, I can feel that. To all the loved ones that show up and hold space with you, even if it means just being there and not saying a thing, I'm with you. I'm with all of you.

As a supporter, I can relate to the fact that there are some super awkward and uncomfortable moments and that sometimes saying nothing is the best thing.

I can relate to the fact that cancer is painful for more than just the patient and that it's really difficult to grasp the fact that we can't fix it.

I can relate to intentionally avoiding asking the question, "How are you feeling?" Because we know the answer won't be what we want to hear. And I can also relate to asking the question anyway in hopes that maybe they are having a good day.

I can relate to the fact that the doctors' offices all feel the same, smell the same, and that for some reason they all have HGTV on in the lobby. I can relate to the fact that I don't care to ever watch HGTV again.

I can relate to the fact that you're tired of hearing your person's name called back for treatment. And I can relate to the fact that you may have started ignoring the "Patient Only" signs. I'm with you. I can relate.

I can relate to the fact that each time the phone rings, you fight the urge to hover over your person to find out what news may have just come in. And you realize it's unnecessary because you can tell pretty quickly by the look on their face what's being said on the other end of the line.

I can relate to the fact that some of your friends are super proactive in reaching out, and some have withdrawn. And I can relate to the fact that either way, it's ok because this is really uncomfortable and awkward for them too.

I can relate to the fact that sometimes you have to be a mom, a dad, a nurse, a spouse, a therapist, a teacher, and a pastor all within the same afternoon.

I can relate to the fact that you're exhausted and need some sleep. And I understand exactly why you'd never even think about voicing that in times like these.

I can relate to the fact that you'll get all kinds of "magic cures" sent to your inbox, and you get to decide which ones to pass on to your loved one and which ones to keep to yourself. I can also relate to the fact that some of them are so outlandish that you're wondering how to even respond to this person without just telling them that it's the stupidest thing you've ever heard of.

I can relate to all the medical bills stacking up on the kitchen counter and trying to sift through what you'll need to pay and what your insurance will pick up. And I can relate to the confusion that comes with all of that.

I can relate to the fact that most times you feel like you have to be the rock, but sometimes you've got nothing left to give. And that that's ok. I hope you know that it's ok to not be ok all the time.

I can relate to the fact that hours go by in your day when you can't remember doing a single productive thing because you're literally in a state of numbness and don't know how to snap out of it.

I can relate to the fact that you begin to think worst possible scenerios. But you know you shouldn't, because you need to stay positive all the time. I can relate.

No, I cannot relate to having cancer. No, I cannot relate to being the patient. No, I cannot relate to my name being called for appointment after appointment, over and over again.

But I can relate to wishing every single day that it was my name they called…instead of theirs.

"YOU DON'T HAVE TO BE THE PERFECT CHRISTIAN."

It was November 20, 2019, and this was the day that we'd start chemo once again. We knew a little bit more about what to expect this time around, but with chemo, there are still so many uncertainties. What will the side effects be? Will Rachel lose her hair again? How sick will it make her? Will it even work?

For those that haven't been through it, chemo isn't fun. But sometimes chemo works. And for that reason, all the uncertainties are worth it. It worked for us the last time, so we were going to assume it would work this time as well. But just because it worked last time doesn't mean it was fun to go through it. I hated chemo days. But the truth is that the chemo wasn't the problem. The chemo was trying to be the solution. It was cancer that was the problem. And it was cancer that I hated most.

Throughout the "cancer chapter" of our lives, we had so many people love us so well. There are so many awesome stories to tell about so many incredible people. And one day, I may just do that. But for now, I just want to share a couple of them. And I'm not going to get into the people behind these words. Instead, I'm just going to focus on the words themselves. Because these words matter.

The first was in a text I received from my friend Greg the day that we found out that the cancer had come back. And here is what he wrote:

"Brandon, I'm praying for you and Rachel today. I know this isn't what you guys were expecting this season of your lives to look like. I know that this doesn't make any sense. I know that

right now, at this moment, this is a surprise to you and that it caught you off guard. But I need you to know that this was not a surprise to our Father and that this did not catch Him off guard. Not even a little bit. Love you, buddy."

And the second was during a conversation with my friend Jennifer on November 20th, the day we'd start chemo again. And she reminded me:

"Brandon, you don't have to be the perfect Christian through all of this. It's ok to be angry. It's ok to be confused. You don't have to keep it all together. No one is expecting perfection from you. And it's even ok to wonder why."

Both of these were so important for Rachel and me to hear as we were entering into another season of uncertainty. Maybe as you're reading this book, you find yourself in a similar season. Maybe for you, it's not cancer, but it's something else you or someone you love is battling. Addiction. Divorce. Depression. Infertility. Loss of a job. Financial strain. The list goes on and on. The truth is that we are all dealing with something. And if for some reason we're not, something is probably coming. So no matter what hard you're going through or no matter what hard is yet to come, I want to take a moment to encouragement you the ways my friends encouraged me:

1. None of this surprised our Father.

2. You don't have to be the perfect Christian.

I can't even begin to explain to you how many times in my life I've gone back to the fact that none of this surprised our Father. No matter how unprepared I may have been, no matter how little sense it made to me at the time, no matter how confusing and scary it was in the moment, none of it was a surprise to Him.

And as for the simple reminder that I didn't have to be the perfect Christian, it was so refreshing. I mean, I knew that I was far from that person, but it was still so nice to hear that it was ok to feel the way I was feeling. Despite what we may have learned in Sunday School, it's possible to have all the faith in the world yet still wonder why.

I wondered why she had to be in constant pain.

I wondered why she wasn't getting better.

I wondered why the treatments weren't working.

I wondered why the cancer came back so quickly in the first place.

I wondered why the kids had to see their mommy sick.

I wondered why her parents had to see their daughter sick.

I wondered why we had other friends going through the same thing.

I wondered why anyone had to go through the same thing.

Every single day, I wondered.

I wondered why.

And because I wondered about all of those things, I felt at times it made me less of a Christian. But that reminder from that sweet friend helped me understand that just because I wondered, it didn't make me bad person. Because I wondered those things, it didn't cause Him to love me any less. Because that's not how it works, and that's not who He is.

Maybe there have been situations in your life where you've had the same wonders? Heck, maybe you're feeling that way at this very moment. I'm just here to encourage you and let you know that it's ok, and it doesn't make you any less of a Christian. He doesn't love us less when we wonder. He knows that we are far from perfect. He just chooses to love us through all of our imperfections. His love is not conditional. His love is perfect, so we don't have to be.

BALDER DOESN'T MEAN SICKER

Hey, quick question: Have you ever walked in on your sister shaving your wife's head? Or *anyone* shaving your wife's head, for that matter?

Well, I did. And it wasn't even awkward at all. Because that's what cancer looks like some days.

The first time we got cancer, the kids and I built "Rachel's Salon" on our back patio and had a head-shaving party.

This second time, we didn't make a big fuss about it. Rachel was just tired of watching it fall out and asked my sister if she'd come over and shave it off. So she did. Because when someone has cancer and asks you to come over and shave their head, you show up, and you shave their head!

This is the period in the cancer journey when the words of affirmation begin to fly around, sounding a lot like this:

"It's just hair."

"It's no big deal; it'll grow back."

"It's a temporary trade-off for getting better."

And though all those things may be true, you don't quite understand that it's more than just hair until it's your family going through it. It's deeper than that. If you knew Rachel, you knew that she was the farthest thing on the planet from being vain. But choosing to be bald for the second time in two years probably wasn't something on her to-do list.

Yes, it was just hair. We knew that. But losing it was a 24/7 reminder to everyone we came in contact with, stranger or not, that we were battling cancer. We may have just as well carried a big sign, announcing to the world, "Hey, look at us, we are sick."

What some people may have a hard time grasping is that balder doesn't mean sicker. But balder does mean inviting everyone else to know you're sick. And for Rachel, that was the worst part about losing her hair. It was never the bald part that was hard for her; it was the sick part. And for some reason, people always seem to equate balder with sicker. And when people thought she was sicker, they began to treat her differently.

Conversations were different. People would talk quieter. Almost like it would hurt her if they spoke too loudly. She missed people talking to her in a normal voice, like a normal adult.

Looks were different. The way people would look at her when she walked into a room was different. There were lots of stares, and you could always tell that people felt sorry for her. For the kids. For us. She missed being able to walk into a room and light it up. We all missed that. That's what she did her entire life, and balder took that away from her.

Hugs were different. If you knew Rachel, you knew she loved hugs. She missed people hugging her like they used to. She missed good, hard, and almost uncomfortably long hugs. Those were her favorite, and she missed them. She was a professional hugger, and she missed people hugging her well.

So here is a little advice from someone that watched his person go through this. I can't speak for all cancer patients and their families, but I can speak for one. I can speak for mine. And I'd be willing to bet that most families would agree.

Balder doesn't mean sicker. So, don't be weird. Don't avoid us. Don't worry about hugging us too hard. No need to feel awkward because you think we feel awkward. Trust me, it's more awkward for you than it is for us. Stop making it weird. The lack of hair doesn't feel awkward at all. It actually makes getting ready for the day so much easier. The cancer all over our bodies may feel awkward, but the hair is just hair, remember?

Yes, we like our hair. Yes, we'd rather have it. But what you may not understand is that it's not the cancer that's causing it to fall out. It's the medicine that does that. So when you see us losing our hair, know it's the medicine's fault, and it may even mean that it's working. So in some cases, in many cases, balder may even mean better.

Yes, we have cancer. We had it a few days ago with hair, and we have it today with no hair. But please, next time you see us, just say hi. Just give us a big ole hug. No need to avoid us. That's what makes it weird. And remember, just because we are missing our hair doesn't mean we have more cancer. Heck, it may even mean we have less.

OUR LAST CHRISTMAS?

"There were moments I wondered if this would be our last Christmas together, but it never even crossed my mind that she wouldn't make it to this one."

This came from a conversation with my friend Andrew, a couple of weeks after his wife passed away and just a month before Christmas 2019. They were our neighbors. He and I would stand at the bus stop each morning, making small talk while waiting for the bus to show up. We did this for an entire year before we realized that both of our wives had cancer. That probably seems strange to you, but I usually don't lead with, "Hey, I'm Brandon. My wife has cancer. How about yours?"

Kinda makes you wonder how many people we come across in our day who may be dealing with something super hard, yet we have no idea. I bet a bunch. For an entire year, I talked with him about football, kids, beer, church, weather, cars, golf, and a bunch of other stuff, but cancer never came up. Until one day, it did.

When we did connect the dots, our morning conversations began to change. We'd ask each other how the appointments were going and how the kids were coping with it all. Small talk about college football turned into big talk about treatment plans and which doctors we liked and which ones we didn't. Our wives became quick friends and were happy to have someone that could understand what the other was going through. They hated what brought them together, but they were glad to get to know each other.

It sounded like treatment was going well for them, and his wife seemed to be getting better. At least, that's what we all thought. Or maybe that's what we all wanted to think. Sometimes, with cancer, I found that what you want to believe is happening and what is actually happening can be two very different things. Needless to say, we wanted to think she was getting better. We thought she was. Until one day, she wasn't.

I found out the news before Rachel did because she was taking a nap when it happened. I found out the news before their kids did because they were at school when their mommy died. They got on the bus that morning, having no idea what would be waiting for them when they got off that afternoon.

I hated having to tell Rachel what I knew. But when I did, she just kept saying, "No. No. No. This can't be true. No. Please no." She had spoken to her 24 hours prior. And she seemed fine then. We thought she was ok. But now she was gone.

I watched his kids get off the bus that afternoon, giddy, smiling, and happy to be home. My heart broke knowing what they were going home to. I watched my kids get off the bus that afternoon the same way. Giddy, smiling, and happy to be home. And my heart broke imagining one day they could be in the exact same shoes, going home to the exact same news.

Up until the day that my buddy's wife passed away, I could relate to a ton of what he had been through.

They had 3 kids. Just like us.

She had breast cancer. Just like us.

She beat it once. Just like us.

Then it came back. Just like us.

But on that day, on the day that she died, I could no longer relate. I couldn't relate to becoming a single dad overnight. I couldn't relate to having to tell my kids that their mommy had died. I couldn't relate to navigating my own grief while at the same time navigating it for three children. I couldn't relate to planning a funeral for the person I was supposed to spend the rest of my days with. I couldn't relate to doing Christmas alone. I couldn't relate to trying to figure out what to do with her presents under the tree.

I could relate to so much of what he'd been through, but just like that, in an instant, I could no longer relate to anything he was going through.

From the moment that she died, the thoughts of, "What if this is our last Christmas together?" became more real to me. I don't know how to explain it. When Rachel's cancer came back, we understood that death was a possibility, but the day our friend passed away, everything felt different. Maybe it just hit a little too close to home. But that was the first day that I really began to think about life without Rachel. And though I knew that I couldn't relate to what my friend was going through, I was scared to death that I may soon have to.

Losing somebody is really hard. Losing somebody around Christmas probably stings a little differently. The holidays have this incredible ability to amplify the relationships that we have, or in some cases, that we don't have. And for those who have lost loved ones, every jingle, every commercial, every mistletoe, every Christmas tree, every billboard, and every Mariah Carey song can be a reminder of what (and who) we have or don't have.

I remember having almost a sense of numbness sweep over me for a few days after Andrew's wife passed away. And I also remember the exact moment I snapped out of it. It was at the grocery store when I saw a couple arguing over a ham. I kid you not; they were in the middle of Kroger, having a heated argument over ham. One wanted ham, the other wanted turkey, and the entire store knew who wanted what. All I could think at that moment was that I bet my friend would love to eat the ham with his wife this Christmas. Or the turkey. It wouldn't matter. I don't even know if he likes ham, but I can promise you, if that's what she wanted, he would have given anything to eat the ham.

I don't know what it is about the holidays, but it's so easy to get wrapped up in all the hustle and bustle that we forget about what and who matters most. Instead, we put the weight of the world on our shoulders and focus on all of the things that won't matter come next week. We set unrealistic expectations for ourselves and for everyone around us, and we try way too hard to do way too much.

For some of us, that may look like prepping extravagant meals or decorating the home to perfection. For others, it may mean making sure the kids look impeccable at church and wrapping the gifts so beautifully that the kids best not even think about touching them. We spend so much time, effort, and energy trying to make Christmas look great on Instagram to complete strangers that we neglect to make it look great for those that matter most.

My friend didn't know that last Christmas would be his wife's last Christmas. The thought had crossed his mind, but he didn't know for sure. We didn't know if Christmas 2019 would be our last Christmas. The thought had crossed our minds, but we didn't know for sure.

And while we are being honest, you don't know if this Christmas will be your last Christmas. I know you don't think it will be, but you just can't know. None of us can. We can't know if it's the last for our mom, our dad, our sister, our brother, our best friend, and even our children. We just can't know for sure. So just trust me when I say this. Treat this Christmas like it's your last Christmas. We don't get do-overs. And none of us are promised another one. So please treat this one that way. I can promise you that you'll never regret doing so.

So do me a favor and consider this: What if you knew this would be your last Christmas? Your last Christmas Eve. Your last Christmas morning. Your last Christmas tree. The last time you get to visit Santa with your kids. If you knew that everything would change over the next year and that this would be your last, how would it look different for you this year?

I bet you'd be more present, not just in proximity but in presence. I bet you'd put your phone down, turn off the TV, forget about work for a while, and actually be with your people. I'd bet you'd even be there with your whole face.

I bet you'd be more generous. Sure, maybe you'd buy more things for more people. But that's not what I mean. I bet you'd be more generous with your time. Because if you knew this was your last, all you'd long for is more time with those you love the most. And I'm certain that you wouldn't take a single second for granted.

I bet you'd eat more food. And maybe even drink more wine. I bet you'd forget about the diet you were on and realize that life is too short for that tomfoolery. You may even remind yourself and those around you that scripture even tells us this.

"So go eat your food and enjoy it; drink your wine and be happy, because that is what God wants you to do." – Ecclesiastes 9:7 (NCV)

I bet you'd be more grateful. Sure, you'd be grateful for the gifts you receive. But that's not what I mean. I bet there would come a moment when you'd look around the room, surrounded by all those that you love, and realize how grateful you are for each and every one of them. Their laugh, their touch, their smell, and all the memories you've shared with them. You'd be grateful that they are still here. And I hope at that moment you'd realize that this would be the perfect time to let them know just how grateful you are for them. Because they are still here and because you still can.

And finally, I bet you'd eat the ham. Even if you don't like it. I'm certain you'd eat the ham.

THE 39

THE INVITATION

I knew that eventually we were going to get to this section of the book. And I wasn't quite sure how I was going to feel about it. I went back and forth with how I wanted to share what I'm about to share. This part is hard. This part hurts. This part isn't the most fun part. But this part matters. It matters a ton. So here is where I landed.

I want to invite you into our room.

While we were in the hospital, and even after Rachel died, I heard from so many people that they wished they could have been in her room. Even if it were just for a moment. They just wanted to watch what was happening in there. Because there was something different going on in there. And people wanted to know what was going on. Those that knew her and those that she'd never met all had one thing in common, they all just wanted to be in that room.

So this is me, inviting y'all in. No, really, I'm inviting you into the room. I want you to spend the next 39 days with us.

I must confess that this is an impossible task and that I'm not a good enough writer to do it justice, but I'm going to try my best. It would be selfish for me to keep it to myself. So that's what I'm going to do. I'm going to try my best.

And though I'm inviting you in, the door is always open. You don't need an invitation. You just needed to show up.

I hope you'll show up.

ROOM 444

January 22, 2020: Day 1

We spent last night in the ER.
Again.

The visitor rules don't apply to us anymore. We've spent way too many nights here for the rules to apply. It seems we've attained platinum or diamond status. Whatever it is, it's a status that we don't care to have. But we do. So we will use it. So come on in. Whenever you'd like. You don't need permission. Come as you are.

Just look for room 444.

I wish I could tell you that things were getting better. I wish I could tell you that I felt really good about our progress. But I gotta be honest with you. Things aren't getting better. They are actually getting much worse. Each day, they seem to be getting worse.

Over the last 72 hours, we've learned that not only does Rachel have cancer in her spinal fluid, but they've also found tumors in her brain.

A simple Google search can tell you how bad the prognosis is:

Medically, we have been told that our time is short.

Medically, we have been told that this can't be cured.

Medically, we have been sentenced to death.

I know this isn't the news that you came here for. I know you've been praying for something different. I know that this doesn't make sense. I know that this doesn't seem fair. Believe me, I have been wrestling with God the last few days because

I felt that He had an awesome opportunity to pull off a miracle while so many people were watching.

I hate seeing her hurt like this. There are no words for how it makes me feel to watch this happen to her.

I begged and pleaded with God to make her better. To heal her. I've asked over and over again for a miracle. And it's not just me doing that. It's you and so many others as well.

And it would be really easy for us to sit here now and be angry. Angry at God for not listening to our prayers. For not fixing this. Believe me, I'm guilty. I've been there. I've had those moments. Many of them.

But I want you to understand when I say this to you, He is working here. He reminded me the other day that there were two answers to all the prayers we've prayed for Rachel, "Yes and Yes."

"Yes, she will be healed. Yes, there will be no more pain. Yes, I'm taking care of her. Yes, I'm performing miracles that you cannot even begin to fathom. My answer is yes. It may not be the yes you were looking for, and I may just bring her home with Me. But My answer is yes. I know you don't understand. But I need you to trust in Me with all your heart and not lean on your understanding, but instead lean on Me. Because I have the ability to make this crooked situation straight."

One of Rachel's biggest fears in all of this is that people will turn from Jesus. Because from the outside looking in, it would be easy to say that He didn't fix this. Guys, that couldn't be farther from the truth. Please don't turn from Him. He is fixing this.

I need y'all to understand that we are not giving up. We start radiation again tomorrow and we are not even thinking about quitting. And though medically we may not have a shot, "miracly" we do. I realize that "miracly" may not be a word, but you know what I mean. It means that we still believe that "miracly," He can make all things right.

And He may just pull that off. But if not, if He brings Rachel home, her eternal home, know that she's ready. We've been able to have some of the most incredible healing conversations these past few days. Rachel is helping us all heal while she's still here. There is an entire story there about that. And it's beautiful.

This is the hardest chapter we've ever faced. There are tears flowing constantly. There is nothing easy about this. The conversations that we are having are so difficult. But Rachel continues to inspire us all to seek Him more, love more like He does, and strive to be more like Him.

I don't know what today or tomorrow holds. But I know that we will be holding her tight and loving her hard until the only one that loves Rachel more than we do brings her home.

"YOU'RE WELCOME FOR GETTING CANCER"

January 25, 2020: Day 4

Yep, we are still here. The hospital is our home for now. We may not be going anywhere for a while. But if y'all think we are just sitting here waiting to die, y'all are crazy.

As you can see, this room is filled with so much dang love.

You may have noticed the walls look a little different. Well, the kids decorated today. Most of the rooms you'll pass on the way in are just plain white. Not this room. Not room 444.

It's impossible for any of us to even begin to comprehend the impact that Rachel is having all across the world - even in these moments.

And I can promise you that each day is filled with its own really special moments.

Some of these moments are really stinkin' hard.

But so many are just so good.

There is so much healing taking place during these moments.

I hate that cancer has given us these moments, but at the same time, as weird as it may sound, I'm so thankful that we get to have some of these moments.

I wish you could hear the conversations that Rachel is having with people. With the doctors, the nurses, the janitors, friends, and with complete strangers that she summons from the hallways. Not that anyone is trying to, but no one can avoid a conversation with Rachel. She's bringing you in. She's inviting you to take a seat at the edge of her bed. And then she'll ask how you're doing. You'll try to turn the conversation to her, but she won't let you. She just wants to know what's happening in your life, and she's going to encourage you in ways you didn't know possible.

You'll enter the room expecting to find someone who's dying, but you'll realize pretty quickly how much she's living. She's living each moment to the fullest, giving everything she has to each person she encounters. And it's beautiful.

Some of my very favorite moments happen in the middle of the night, as I'm holding her hand and listening to her breathe. I love the sound of her breathing. I didn't know how much I loved that sound until I was told that it may not last much longer. I'm just not prepared for that to stop yet. That's my biggest prayer. I just keep praying that I can listen to her breathing for another day.

At about 11 p.m. last night, after everyone had left for the evening, I settled into my spot next to her bed to listen to her breathe. She opened her eyes, looked into mine, and asked me;

"Babe, how many people have read your blog post now?"

"Last I looked, almost 800,000," I replied.

With a little grin on her face, as her tired eyes began to close, she joked yet again, "You're welcome for getting cancer so you could go viral."

CHIEFS 4 RACH

February 2, 2020: Day 12

Over the past 24 hours, people have flown in from Arizona, Texas, Nebraska, Washington, Illinois, New York, and Missouri.

And the crazy part is that they have all come for a football game. No, the football game isn't taking place in Knoxville. It's actually in Miami. But Rachel is in Knoxville, and everyone wants to watch this particular game with her. So they all came here instead.

They all came here to watch the Super Bowl with Rachel.

Now that I think about it, they all came here to watch Rachel watch the Super Bowl.

This had never happened before in her life. Her favorite team, the Kansas City Chiefs had actually been pretty terrible for most of her life. But not this year. This year they were different. This year they were great.

Most of those that came couldn't care less about the game. Some of them didn't even like football. Most of them didn't have a dog in the fight. But the game mattered to Rachel, so they came. There was no invite. They didn't ask for permission. They just showed up. And they all wore red.

And though it would have been nice to break Rachel out for the day to go somewhere fun, that wasn't possible. So instead of checking her out, everyone just checked themselves in.

My brother found a projector so we could have a big screen projecting off the wall in room 444. The nurses made some of Rachel's favorite side dishes. My buddies RJ and Big Brandon rolled the keg in. My parents got the balloons. One of Rachel's friends owns a boutique in Kansas City and sent the party favors and t-shirts. No one showed up empty-handed, and this party quickly became the talk of the hospital.

The Chiefs were down 20-10 with about seven minutes left in the game. Things were not looking good at all. The room had gotten pretty quiet, and a few people were even making their rounds saying their goodnights. I didn't know what else to do, so I just began to pray. Yes, I realize that God didn't care about the outcome of the game. Yes, I understand He had bigger things on his plate. Yes, as I was praying for the Chiefs, it felt useless. But if there were ever a game that I thought He may just intervene in, it was this one. Not because he hates the 49ers but because He loves Rachel and because she loves the Chiefs.

And believe it or not, He did. Over the final 6 minutes of the game, the Chiefs' offense came alive and scored 21 unanswered points to win the game. The room got so loud that it began to shake. It felt as if we were actually at the game. We woke up the entire floor and probably ticked off a ton of people. But at that moment, as Rachel had her hands in the air singing "Red Kingdom," we didn't care. Not even a little bit. We were the champs, and Rachel got to see her team win the Super Bowl in what may have been the final game she'd ever see.

We weren't at the stadium watching the game from the 50-yard line. We weren't watching it on our big screen in the comfort of our own home. We weren't at the bar with thousands of others celebrating the Super Bowl victory. We were in the hospital. In room 444. With a bunch of people that just decided to show up. Not because we asked them to. Not because we expected them to. But because it's what they wanted to do. So they did. And it was perfect.

"WHO'S GOT HER?"

February 5, 2020: Day 15

"Each night when we come to work, all us nurses gather around and ask, 'Who's got her?' And we all know who 'her' is."

That's what one of the nurses said last night as a few of us watched Rachel sleep. We do that a lot. We just sit and watch her sleep. Sometimes we'll talk to each other. Sometimes not a word is spoken. We just sit and watch her.

Hearing the nurse say that isn't a huge surprise, but it's still so sweet to hear. Rachel has done this for her entire life. Wherever she goes she makes an impact. And even in her death, she seems to be doing exactly the same.

It isn't just the nurses, but the doctors too. Doctors come in on their days off to see her. They sneak her ice cream sandwiches and serenade her on their guitars. The cleaning staff. The admins. The Chaplin. They all know who "her" is, and anyone that gets the opportunity to help take care of her leaves the room better than when they entered.

This isn't normal. I can assure you that this isn't happening in other rooms. Or in other hospitals.

This is so special. She is so special.

I'm so glad that "her" is mine.

I'm so glad that "her" loves so well.

I'm so glad that we all get to love "her" back.

One of Rachel's biggest concerns with everything going on isn't her cancer. It's not the pain she's constantly in. It's not all the uncertainty. It's the fact that she never wants to be a burden on anyone and that right now, she feels like she's a burden on everyone. She hates that she needs help to go to the bathroom. She hates that she needs to call a nurse just to get out of bed. She hates that she has to rely on anyone to help her do anything and constantly feels like she's a burden.

I told her that was a stupid thing to think. And that it was an even stupider thing to say out loud. Because she's not a burden now and has never been a burden to anyone. I probably could have handled it better than calling her thoughts and words stupid. But that's all I could think of. Because to me, it's stupid.

All that to say, that's who Rachel is, and that's how she lives. It's not about her. It's never about her. It's always about everyone else.

Gosh, I'm so glad that we all got "her."

MOMMY WITH JESUS = DADDY WITH US

February 10, 2020: Day 20

There have been a whole lot of hard days in the hospital, but this one has to be in the running for one of the hardest. Today is the day that I have to tell our kids that their mommy isn't going to be coming home.

I knew eventually I was going to have to have this conversation with them. I knew that it wasn't going to be easy. I've dreaded this day from the moment I found out that Rachel wouldn't be coming home.

It wasn't a secret to our kids that Rachel wasn't getting better. They understood that she may go to Heaven sooner than later. We didn't hide the fact that things weren't going well. But to have to say these words. To have you sit your kids down on a couch in a hospital lobby and utter these words. It's really hard. And I pray that none of you ever have to experience this.

Yes, parents are supposed to die before their kids do. But no, parents aren't supposed to die when their kids are still kids.

I didn't sleep at all last night knowing that I was going to have this conversation with them today. This just isn't fair to them. They aren't supposed to lose their mommy this young. Mommies are supposed to be there to help their kids navigate through all the milestones that come with growing up. My girls remind me all the time that mommies are just better than daddies at some things. Lots of things. And my girls are so right. That's not just their opinion. That's a fact.

My sister Taylor volunteered to accompany me to have this conversation with them. And I'm so glad she did because I knew that I couldn't do this alone - just like so many other things that I'd be facing down the road. So after their daily visit to see mommy, we took them down to the lobby and told them we wanted to chat with them for a minute.

They just stared at me, waiting for me to say something. And I lost it. I couldn't get a word out. And once they saw me crying, they started crying. So there we are, in the middle of the hospital lobby, bawling our eyes out.

Eventually, I found some words and told them that Mommy wasn't going to be coming home but that she gets to go to Heaven instead. And that when mommy goes to Heaven, daddy gets to come home.

We all hugged and cried. No more words were spoken. Nothing else needed to be said. We just held onto each other.

And then, after a few minutes, Hadley squeezed me as tight as she could, and through her tears, she said, "It's ok, daddy, we understand. We are just ready for you to come home now."

I haven't been home in about 20 nights. They just want me to come home. They know that mommy will be ok, but now it's clear to them that when daddy comes home, it means mommy is in Heaven. And that is good. Because that means mommy is with Jesus and daddy can be with them.

'TIL DEATH DO US PART

February 13, 2020: Day 23

Gosh, this week has been really hard. I wish I had some great news to share with you. I wish I could tell you that we've turned a corner and that things are getting better. I wish I could tell you that we were encouraged by something. But that's just not where we are. That's just not the case.

I guess if we are being honest, all the days have felt different lately. Between you and me, we've even said our goodbyes a few times. That's right, there have been three different times that we thought she was gone and wasn't coming back. Three different times I said goodbye to her. Just last night, she had a seizure that lasted way too long, and the doctors were certain that she wouldn't come out of it. They pulled me aside and told me that there was no way she could survive this. Until she did. They told me that her brain certainly wouldn't be functioning properly anymore. Until it was.

I kid you not. There were about 12 of us in the room, praying over her, saying our goodbyes, when out of nowhere, she opened her eyes, looked at me, and said, "I need to pee."

I can't make this stuff up. And I have 11 other witnesses to validate this happened. It didn't make any sense. Medically speaking, there was no way she should have come out of it. They told me that she had been gone for way too long. Until she wasn't gone anymore and she needed to pee.

We just can't believe what's happening. The doctors can't seem to make any sense of it. It's not that she's getting better, but she just keeps hanging on. They keep telling me that it's not supposed to happen this way. That she should be gone. That there is no way she should be in the room right now eating strawberries and welcoming visitors. But as you can see, that's exactly where she is, and that's exactly what she is doing.

We've been in this hospital for 23 days now. And I bet we've welcomed 150 visitors. Each day, someone new walks into room 444, and each person fills Rachel's bucket up a little bit more. Maybe that's why she keeps hanging on. Maybe that's why she's not quite ready to say goodbye. Maybe it's because all of you just keep showing up. Thank you so much for showing up. Please don't stop showing up.

And please understand we realize not everyone can just show up. We understand that people have responsibilities, kids, work, and so many other things going on in their lives. We realize that everyone has their own hard that they are dealing with. This just happens to be ours right now. We know you'd love to be here, but we also know that some of you can't. And that's the main reason why I share so openly.

Sharing what's going on in here has been so good for me, and I hope it's helped you as well. I know that many of you would love to stop everything else you have going on in your life to come and see Rachel. To say your goodbyes. I get it. We all get it. But I promise we understand, and I promise you I'll keep sharing.

Rachel reminded me today that we are exactly one month away from our 10th wedding anniversary. She also reminded me that we were supposed to go to Hawaii to celebrate. And then she said, "I'm sorry, babe, it doesn't look like that's going to happen this year."

For better, for worse, for richer, for poorer, in sickness and in health, to love and to cherish, 'til death do us part…

Nearly 10 years ago, Rachel and I stood in front of hundreds of loved ones and exchanged those words. We may have added some flair into our vows, like the promise of endless candy in the pantry and unlimited back rubs, but the "for better or worse" part meant the most.

And boy, have we lived up to those vows. I mean, she's always stayed by my side and supported me at my worst. And believe me when I say that I've had a lot of "worse." A whole bunch of "worse." She was my number one supporter during our "poorer." And believe me when I say that we've seen some poorer. She never wavered, never faltered, never gave up on me — no matter how bad things may have gotten. She was always willing to pick me up when I'd fall. She deserved so much better, but for some reason, she chose me. And she just kept showing up.

I remember our wedding day like it was yesterday, and thinking that the "'til death do us part" would come someday. Never in a million years did I think that "part" would come so soon. That "part" was supposed to happen 50 or 60 years from now. Not any day now. But as I sit here today, watching her sleep in the same hospital room we've been living in for almost a month, that "part" is exactly what we're facing.

As of now, the main goal is to keep her as comfortable as possible. And they've done that. She's more comfortable than she's been in months. She doesn't have pain like she once did. The "cocktail of medicine" they have her on is doing the trick. And if it weren't for her short-term memory loss and random seizures, there are times you'd wonder what we're even doing in this hospital.

Each morning, when she wakes up (could be 3 a.m., could be 8 a.m., could be 11 a.m.), she asks me — and whoever else happens to be in the room — the same question:

"What's the plan for today?"

And each morning, my response is the same. For almost four weeks, my response hasn't changed.

I ask her if she's comfortable. She says, "yes."

I ask her if she has any pain. She says, "no."

And then I say, "that's perfect," and reassure her that the plan is working. That she's doing an awesome job with the plan.

She smiles and says, "good."

I love that smile so much.

I assume she asks this each day because she's forgotten that there isn't a plan. That we aren't going anywhere. That we are literally just waiting. Waiting for her to die. But other days, I bet she just hopes. Hopes that the plan has changed. That maybe today is the day we'll bust out of this place.

I'll never again hear that question the same way.

"What's the plan for today?"

I dread it each morning because I hate my answer so much. I wish I could offer her more clarity. I wish I could tell her that things were getting better. Or that eventually, they will get better. I wish I could encourage her by telling her that we're heading home any day now. I wish I could fix this. But I can't do any of those things.

We have come to a really awkward point in our journey. There are no more treatment plans. The doctors have exhausted all their options. At this point, we just wait.

And I know each day that passes is one day closer to me losing Rachel. One day closer to our three kids losing their mommy. To her parents losing their only daughter. To my sister losing not only her sister-in-law but her best friend. To her brother losing his sister. To my mom and dad, to all of our family, to her friends, and to those who know her from afar, all grieving the fact that we are losing such a beautiful person.

As ugly as this all sounds, she's continued to have an enormous impact on so many people. As one friend put it the other day, "I don't even think we've begun to see where she may take us."

These days are so hard. But in all the pain and suffering, between the tears and the fear, there is something so beautiful happening.

"People come to this room to be ministered to," is what her dad said to me the other day. And when Rachel overhead this, her response was perfect.

"I know that I'm dying. I am at peace with that. And all I have left to give is Jesus."

I'm not simply watching my wife die. That would be terrible and unbearable. I'm watching her live and love in a way that is beyond beautiful. I'm watching her minister to the masses. Each day, I have a front-row seat to something indescribable. You can't comprehend it unless you're here.

I'm watching doctors and nurses in tears as Rachel shares stories with them about what she's feeling and where she's heading. And then I get to watch Rachel reassure them that it's going to be ok.

I'm watching friends flock in from all over the world just to spend five minutes with her, and I'm watching her comfort each and every one of them before they leave.

Every single day, I watch as people come to say their goodbyes. And though you'd think it would be a brutal thing to watch, what I see is people who enter the room one way and leave the room completely transformed.

I can't explain it. It's something you'd have to experience to understand. But it's beautiful. There is so much beauty in the brokenness. And Rachel has helped us all find the beauty.

I have no idea how much longer we have. And we still have hope that Jesus will fix this. We've never wavered from that. But we'd be crazy if we didn't recognize all the miracles that He is performing right in front of our eyes, every day, through Rachel's story. Not just in this hospital room but all around the world.

If you've never met Rachel, I'm really sorry. I hate that for you. I wish you could all have just five minutes with her. I promise you'd look at life in a completely different way. I promise you that you'd enjoy the everyday moments so much more. I promise you that you'd complain less and laugh more. If you could just have five minutes with her, you'd understand what loving others really looks like. You'd leave so much better, and you'd love so much harder.

I'm so glad she chose me nearly 10 years ago to walk this walk with her. I'm so glad she chose me to fight this fight with her. I'm so glad she never gave up on me. And as ugly as this chapter should be, I'm just so glad she picked me. Every single day I'm grateful that she chose me. Our story is my favorite love story.

'Til death do us part.

I LOVE YOU MORE THAN CONSTRUCTION SITES

February 14, 2020: Day 24

Macklin loves construction sites. There really isn't anything that brings him more joy. The noises. The tractors. The bulldozers. The excavators. The wrecking balls. He could sit and watch construction sites all day long. His favorite book of all time is called "Construction Site on Christmas Night." And it happens to be a book we read every night. He is all boy, and he can't get enough of construction sites.

With today being Valentine's Day, Macklin knew exactly what he wanted to make his mommy. He worked so hard on it and couldn't wait to deliver it to her today.

Macklin is five years old. Macklin knows how to love. He doesn't just say it; he shows it.

For the majority of Mack's life, Rachel has been sick. And for the majority of that time, Mack has been right by her side.

The good days. The not-so-good days. The really hard days. Even the days that Rachel spent on the bathroom floor. He'd just show up. He'd feed her snacks. He'd lay by her side. He'd rub her back. He'd serve her the best way that he knew how. Most of the time, that just meant being there. By her side. Looking for nothing in return.

Each day for the past 24 days, when Macklin comes to the hospital, he crawls into Rachel's bed with her. It doesn't matter if she's asleep or awake. It doesn't matter if the doctors are in the room or not. It doesn't matter to him what else is going on. He doesn't need to be entertained. He doesn't make a sound. He's not there to be noticed. He doesn't need an invitation. He just shows up.

Macklin knows that he can't fix his mommy. He understands that he can't make her better. So he shows his love for Rachel in the best way that he knows how. Through the ministry of presence.

THE LAST FIELD TRIP

February 17, 2020: Day 27

I'm losing count, but I think that today marks 27 days of us being here.

Nearly an entire month of hospital food.

A month of trying to sleep through machines that beep all night.

A month of lots of confusion and questions.

A month of patients checking in and checking out.

A month of visitors coming and going.

When we checked in a month ago, we didn't plan to stay this long.

But here we are, 27 days later.

Everyone at the hospital knows who we are. Not because we are "knowable" but because we aren't leaving. Well, Rachel is knowable, but the rest of us have become known because we've been here so long.

We are all here.

We are all waiting.

And everyone knows what we are waiting for.

I don't think they want us to leave. Because once we leave, everyone will know why. And as much as we all want to go home, none of us want to leave.

Remember when I told you that the hospital rules don't apply to Rachel? Well, this morning, my sister-in-law informed the nurses that Rachel would like to go outside. And that whether they like it or not, we are going to take her outside.

Side note: If you ever find yourself in a situation like mine - where you're spending way too many nights in a hospital. Find an advocate. Or two. Or three. Find someone to be your voice and to speak up for your person. I'm so thankful that I had those people. Kim, Taylor, and Ashley, thank you for being those people

Needless to say, we didn't have to twist any arms to go outside that day. The nurses were thrilled to be a part of this, and I even overheard one of them say, "This is so special. I can't believe that we get to take her on her last field trip."

For the first time in 27 days, Rachel was going outside.

She cried the moment the sun touched her face. She threw her hands in the air and wept.

We all cried as we watched her cry.

The kids and her parents showed up to surprise her. The valet guys cheered her on as we came out of the front doors. The nurses rolled out the red carpet and made sure that everything went perfectly.

The weather in Knoxville in February is unpredictable. And what never happens is a 64-degree day. Until it did. Until today.

Rachel got to feel the sunlight on her face. She got to breathe the fresh air in her lungs. And she got to watch her kids play outside for what may have been the final time.

OUR LAST DATE

February 20, 2020: Day 30

This morning when Rachel woke up, after she asked me what the plan was for the day, she said, "I just want a big ol' tub of movie theatre popcorn, a giant coke, and one more date with you."

So, that's what we did. For the first time since we'd checked into the hospital, I asked everyone to give us an evening. Just a couple of hours, really. So we could have one last date. And one last selfie.

I don't think many of us have the opportunity to know when our last date will be. But Rachel and I both knew that this would probably be it for us. There was no hiding where we were at this point. We talked openly about it all. And we were at peace knowing that we were in our final days together.

It turns out that this last date was about more than popcorn and coke. To me, it felt like I'd been set up. And it was obvious that Rachel had some things that she wanted to say before she was gone. I'm not sure when she planned this "date." It could have been months ago; it could have been days ago. But she had plans, and it was all written in the notes section of her phone.

At this point, it was hard for Rachel to say a whole lot and even harder for her to keep her thoughts straight, so she asked me if I could just read them out loud, one at a time.

She had them numbered, and there were eight of them in all:

1.   I want you to find love again. Not tomorrow or in two weeks. That would be weird, and everyone would be talking about you behind your back. But sooner than later. I want you to find love again. This is so important to me. I want you to find someone that will love you like I do. I want you to find someone that will love the kids like I do. I want you to find someone that will root you on in all your crazy ideas. At the same time, I want her to understand that just because I'm gone, it doesn't mean you stop loving me. I want her to know that you'll always love me but that she doesn't have to compete with me. I'm not coming back to take you away from her, and I'll be her biggest fan from up there. But I also want her to know that if she screws this up, if she messes with your heart or my babies, she will feel my wrath. And believe me, she doesn't want that.

2.   I want you to take care of yourself. I need you to understand this. The kids need you around for a really long time. You aren't allowed to be careless with your health. You need to eat better. Tacos, pizza, and soft pretzels aren't an acceptable diet. You need to be proactive. You can't let things linger. If something comes up, you need to get it looked at. You may not love what I'm about to say next, but I've already made you a doctor's appointment for next month. It's booked. You

don't have to do anything but show up. Don't you dare cancel that appointment. Or you'll feel my wrath. You don't want that.

3. I want you to join the golf club with your dad. I know I said we need to pay off our credit card debt first, but when you're on your deathbed, that just doesn't seem that important anymore. What seems most important is spending more time with your dad, doing what y'all love most. That's what matters. Do more of that. Do more of what matters. Do more of what you love. Join the club.

4. I want you to take care of my babies. Gosh, they are lucky to have you as their daddy. Keep being the best daddy you can be. Keep teaching them about Jesus and how good He is. Make sure that they understand that even in the bad, He is so good. Don't let other things distract you from them. They are your priority. Hadley is going to need someone to brush her hair and encourage her in her school work. Do that. Cooper is going to need a dance partner and someone to watch all of her performances. Do that. Macklin is going to need someone to snuggle with and listen to his stories. Do that. And please remind them every single day how much I love them. And make them understand that though I'm not here, I'll always be there. Oh, and I've made hair appointments for the girls. I've already added them to your calendar. I got you.

5. I want you to work less. I know you know how I feel about this. When you're working too much, you don't give us enough. You're not allowed to do that anymore. I need you to understand your limits. I need you to shut it off and be present with your people. I won't be here to remind you of this, so I've invited other people to do that for me. Don't shoot the messengers. It's not them; it's me. We can all tell when your mind is somewhere else Shut it off and be present. Be there with your whole face.

6. I want you to finish your book. You've been talking about it for way too long. People are tired of hearing about it and probably don't even believe you'll do it anymore. Stop talking about it, babe. Stop thinking about it. It's getting old. Please, do me a favor and just do.

7. I want you to know that I'm ok. I really feel like my work here is done. I feel like I've done all I can here, and I'm at peace with the life that I've lived. You're not going to like this either, but I've made sure that lots of people will be looking out for you and the kids. They've told me that they will, and I believe that they will. Not just for a little bit, but I think they will just keep showing up. Let people show up. Let people help you. I know this will be hard for you, but it's what people want to do, and it's what love does. And believe me, you're gonna need lots of help, babe.

8. I want you to know that I love you with all of my heart and that I'm so glad you chose me. I want you to know that I'm so proud of you. I want you to know that I trust you and that I know with all that I am that you'll give the kids the best life imaginable. I want you to understand that there is nothing more you could have done to take the cancer away. I know you think there was, and I know you beat yourself up at times, but you did everything you could. The rest is up to God. I want you to know that you're the best thing that has ever happened to me. And though I wish we had more life to live together, I'm so glad I got to live the rest of mine with you.

I cried. The entire time I read the note, I cried. Rachel was in and out of sleep, so I'm not sure she understood the impact it had on me. It took me much longer than it should have to get through it. I had to take a few breaks. I even stood up and paced back and forth a few times, trying to gain my composure. I'm not sure I saw our last date going this way. I didn't prepare as well as she did. I just showed up. She did the hard stuff.

After a few minutes of silence, I kissed her forehead and thanked her again for choosing me. And she whispered,

"I love you, baby. I'm so tired. I don't think I want to be here anymore. I just want to go home. I'm just ready to go home now."

BECAUSE I LEFT THE ROOM

March 1, 2020: Day 39

My pastor came by yesterday, just like he did most days, and I think he could tell we were close to the end. I'm assuming he's been here a time or two. And though it was a first for me, it wasn't his first time to watch someone die. As I walked him out that evening, he hugged me and said, "I just want you to know that it's ok to be relieved when she's gone."

At first, it kind of shook me. I didn't know pastors could say stuff like that. It didn't seem very "pastorish." I don't know if that's even a word, but you know what I mean. I just didn't expect to hear that from him. But as I was watching Rachel struggle to breathe last night, I began to understand precisely what he meant. And I was so thankful that he gave me that permission. I needed that permission.

He knew exactly what he was talking about. He knew that we were all tired. He knew how much we wanted to go home. He knew that my kids needed their daddy. He knew that Rachel had done her job and done it so well. He knew that something so much better was waiting for her. And that's why he knew that it was ok to give me permission to be relieved when she left.

Today has gone just like most days have this week. Pretty uneventful. And at this point, Rachel isn't interacting anymore. She just sleeps all the time. She is starting to look a little different now. Almost lifeless. Part of me thinks that she may have already gone. She's still breathing, but I'm not sure she's here anymore.

I think we are probably getting close now. I'm not sure how close, but I think this is what close looks like.

I don't leave her room much. I go to the cafeteria once in a while. I walk the halls from time to time. And I go home to shower and check in with the kids every few days. But for most of the last 39 days, you could find me right next to Rach, in room 444.

I've heard people say that your person doesn't want to die with you in the room. That they don't want you to see it. That they just won't let go while you're present. I never believed that. I thought it was just a myth that someone made up along the way.

But that afternoon, when I left...

She died.

I hadn't even left the hospital grounds. I was in the parking lot saying goodbye to my brother, Rachel's parents, and the kids when I got a call from our friend who was keeping watch over Rachel. She told me I needed to run up to her room as fast as I could.

So I did.

And by the time I got there, she was already gone.

The nurses were nice enough to wait for me to be there to announce her time of death at 4:34 p.m.

But if we are being honest, I bet she was gone at 4:31 or 4:32.

Just like they say. Whoever "they" are. She wasn't going to die while I was there. And she didn't. She waited for me to leave.

Everyone cleared the room to let me have some time with Rachel. I talked to her for a bit. But most things had already been said. She was gone. And my pastor was right. I was relieved.

It was at that moment when I truly understood that this meant she would have no more pain. No more uncertainty. There would be no more appointments and no more scans. She would suffer no more. Because on March 1, 2020, at 4:30-something p.m., Rachel beat cancer.

I'm not sure how long I stayed in the room with her. It's all kind of a blur. The nurses were so gracious and allowed me to go at my own pace. I think this was really hard for them too. Rachel was their favorite, and everyone knew that. Maybe it was 30 minutes, maybe it was an hour, I'm not really sure, but eventually, I gave her one last kiss, told her I loved her, thanked her one more time for choosing me, and walked out of that room for the final time.

My brother and my dad were waiting for me. We drove and met my sister and my mom. I don't remember a ton of that time together, but I do remember that it was really sweet.

The kids didn't know at this point. They were at our house with Rachel's parents and were already in bed when I made it home. I chatted with her parents for a few minutes and then went and checked on the kids.

First, there was Macklin, and he woke up when I kissed him on the cheek, "Daddy, you're home!" he said excitedly.

Then it was Cooper's turn. She woke up with a very similar reaction, "Daddy, you're here!"

By the time I made it to Hadley, she was already awake. She just gave me a big hug and said, "Daddy, I'm so glad you're home, and I'm so glad mommy is too."

I was home

Mommy was too.

And I was relieved.

THE NEXT
FEW WEEKS

$2.34

March 3, 2020

I think that I'm a pretty good dad. I think that most days, I can do the dad thing pretty well. I for sure have my bad moments. I definitely lose my patience sometimes. I get frustrated more than I probably should. And I'm far from perfect. But for the most part, I'm a pretty good dad, and it's my favorite thing on the planet to be.

But what I also know is that I'm not a good mom. I've never claimed to be. It was never in my plans to have to be one. I just don't do "mom" well at all. It's the hardest job there is, and I'm far from equipped to do that job.

Rachel, on the other hand, was an incredible mom. Hadley, Cooper, and Macklin were so blessed to get to have her as their mom for the past eight, seven, and five years, respectively.

No one did "mommy" better than she did. I loved watching her be a mom. Watching her "mom" was one of my favorite things to do.

Gosh, she was such a good mom.

Gosh, those kids had it so dang good.

Gosh, I miss her so much.

A few days before Rachel passed away, I came home for a couple hours to give the kids baths and to help them pick out their clothes for school pictures the following day. As I was brushing Cooper's hair after bath time, she said something that I'll never forget:

"Daddy, I just want you to know that you're doing a really good job at mommy things."

For the rest of her life, she'll never know how badly my heart needed to hear that.

Monday, the day after Rachel went to be with Jesus, Cooper gave me this card:

And for a moment, that moment, I realized that we would be ok. That it doesn't matter how good of a mommy I think I am. It doesn't matter how much I lack in the areas that mommy was so good at. It doesn't matter how poor a cook I am or how bad I am at doing hair.

What matters is that Cooper is thankful that I'm her dad and that she thinks I'll be a pretty good mom. I'll take that. I'll take that all day long.

I'm not sure what the $2.34 represents. But I'll take that too.

This is going to be so hard. But we will be ok. And I'm grateful for reminders like this. Reminders that Cooper believes in me, and she believes in me so much that she gave me back what was left over from her allowance.

BURNT EGGS AND HEAD LICE

March 18 2020

I used to love March. March was my jam. March and I were super cool.

Each year in March, Rachel and I would celebrate our anniversary. This year we were supposed to be in Hawaii.

With March comes Spring and everyone loves Spring. It brings warmer weather unless you live in Nebraska. There you'll have to wait 'til June.

March brings March Madness. The greatest sporting event of the entire year.

I used to love March.

Until this March.

Because as y'all know, this March started off with the worst day of my entire life.

And y'all also know, that just a couple of weeks later, on March 13th, the entire country shut down. This was something that Rachel hadn't prepared me for. It's something that she couldn't see coming. I'd heard of this COVID-19 thing while we were in the hospital but it hadn't done it's thing quite yet. Until I got home. And then they shut the schools down. The churches closed their doors. They even had the nerve to cancel March Madness. And then, maybe worst of all, restaurants were no longer open. I can't cook. I don't know how to cook. Rachel cooked. My plan had been to eat out for three meals a day. Until I couldn't. Until we couldn't. Until this March.

But what y'all don't know is that on my very first night home from the hospital in 39 nights, Hadley puked. All over my room.

The bed, the floor, the bathroom, everywhere. For no reason at all. She just puked. She wasn't sick. But she puked anyway. And y'all know that I don't do puke. That was Rachel's thing. Rachel did puke. I had to do puke for the first time in my life that night. It was my first night alone, and I had to do puke.

And also, y'all don't know that a few days ago, Macklin wanted scrambled eggs for breakfast. And since all the dang restaurants were closed, I had to make them on my own. I'd never made scrambled eggs before. Rachel did scrambled eggs. That morning the eggs were on me. And I failed. Macklin said that they were too brown and didn't even taste like eggs.

And, on top of that, yesterday, he got his leg stuck in a table and fell down the stairs all within 15 minutes. He needed Rachel. I'm not good at fixing bumps and bruises and broken egos. Rachel did that. That was her thing. But yesterday it was on me.

And that brings us to today. Today we found out that both Hadley and Cooper have head lice. I don't do head lice. Rachel did head lice. But today, and for the next few weeks, I'm having to do lice.

I'm realizing more and more each day that Rachel did it all. And I'm understanding more and more how well she did it all. I'm learning to do my best even if most times my best falls way short of the way mommy would have done it. I'm trying. I'm not doing a great job with it all. But I'm trying.

It's the puke, and the falls, and the eggs, and the lice that have made me miss her so much this March. Not to mention the piles of laundry and the folding of the fitted sheets. The laundry simply never ends and I don't care what anyone says, those dang fitted sheets just don't fold.

THESE CRIES

March 20, 2020

This is really hard.

They say it gets easier with time. But if I can be honest, so far, it hasn't gotten easier. In fact, it may have gotten harder. I can't explain why, I just know that with each day that passes, I seem to miss her more and more. And I seem to need her more and more.

Most days I find myself sitting on our closet floor, just like I am right now, where I can hide from the kids for 15-20 minutes, and just cry.

It's not that I don't want them to see me cry. Not a day has gone by that we don't cry together.

But these cries are different cries. They aren't just the "I miss her cries." Those happen all the time.

These are the "I'm scared to death of doing life without her," cries.

These are the "how am I supposed to do this on my own," cries.

These are the "this wasn't supposed to happen and I wish it would have been me," cries.

These are the "I can't even hear a song without thinking of you," cries.

These are the "I'm sorry I didn't fight harder, I'm sorry I didn't do more, and I'm sorry that it felt like at times we gave up," cries.

These cries are different cries.

So many things happened during those 39 nights that we spent in the hospital that bring me to these cries. So many things happened in the last 2 years since our original diagnoses that bring me to these cries. So many things happened over the almost 10 years that we were married that bring me to these cries.

I just wish I could have one more hug. I just wish I could have one more conversation. I just wish I could binge-watch "This is Us" with her one more time. I just want to hear her voice. Man, I miss her voice. I just want to see her smile. Gosh, I miss her smile so much. I just want to watch her be "mom" one more time. I just want one more day. One more moment. One more second. Just one more.

THE
WISH

"I WISH WE ALL LIVED LIKE WE HAD IT."

I promised Rachel I was going to finish this book. And I did it.

Well, I'm doing it.

Right now.

I'm writing the last chapter.

So I think it's safe to say that I did it. I don't know that anyone will read it, but that's not the promise I made. I just promised her that I'd write it. The rest is out of my hands.

I hope she is proud of me. I hope she is proud of us. I hope she is bragging on her family up there. I'd like to think that she is.

And I hope she knows how proud of her we are down here. And that we brag on her all the time. I bet she knows that.

I hope this book honors her well. That's why it was written, and I hope the words are good enough to do her life justice. It's not an easy task to write about the best person you've ever known because sometimes words just aren't enough. I just hope these words are enough.

I've had a ton of fun with it. I love to write, and I love to tell stories, especially about Rachel and the kids. And if you think the story of us ends with this book, you've got another thing coming. This is just the beginning. There is so much more to our story. There is so much more to tell. But not today. Not right now.

For now, I need to wrap up this part of our story. Because I told her I would.

Life sure does come at you fast. On March 1, 2018, we didn't have cancer. And on March 1, 2020, cancer took Rachel's life.

I could sit here today and talk about all the things that cancer took from us, but there isn't a chance in the world I'm going to do that. Because if I did, cancer wins. And that's not what happened. I'm not going to let cancer think it won. Because it never had a shot.

Cancer did change our lives. It did rob us of some time. But it wasn't victorious over us.

From the moment that we were diagnosed, we had one focus: to live another day. That's it. It was to wake up and live that day the best that we could.

It's pretty special what occurs when you live your life that way, and it's amazing how the things that once mattered so much begin to not matter at all.

In one of my final conversations with Rachel, she said to me, "I wish we all lived like we had it."

"It," meaning cancer.

And what she meant was that she wished people would live their lives like they didn't have much time left to live. Because to live like that is truly living.

This isn't about cancer. It has nothing to do with cancer. Don't let cancer be the reason you start living. Let living be reason enough for that.

And if Rachel were here today, I think we all know what she would say:

She would tell you to stop what you are doing and go spend time with your people. Because one day, you are going to look up, and they won't be there anymore.

She would encourage you to chase the girl. Even if it takes ten years to convince her that you're the one. And then, once you've caught her, she'd encourage you to keep on chasing after her.

She would remind you to run like crazy toward your wildest dreams. And if that happens to scare you, she'd tell you to grab your Batman costume. Because everything is less scary when you go as Batman.

She would admit that she did, in fact, "wreck it." But that it was just an "it" and that it really doesn't matter that much. She would encourage you to let "it" go. To not let it linger for too long. And remind you that most "its" can be fixed.

She would tell you that the scary-looking man at the grocery store really isn't scary at all. And that he has a name. And that he has a story. And then she would give you the nudge you need to walk up to him and ask, "Who is your name?"

She would let you know that nothing is too small or too big for Jesus to fix. And that He's in the business of doing that. He's the best there ever was at it. So there is no reason in the world not to ask Him to fix it.

She would agree that some people are hard to love but remind you that sometimes we're *all* hard to love. That we aren't perfect and that we don't have to love perfectly. But that we will never regret loving. Even when it's really hard, it's really worth it.

She would remind you to just keep doing. That it shouldn't take cancer, an emergency, or some other diagnosis for you "to do." That you have the opportunity to show up and do every day. It doesn't require money. It doesn't require gifts. It doesn't even require any talent or special skills. It's easier and harder than it seems. It's easier because we can all do it. It's harder because it demands our time. Even when we are tired. Even when it feels uncomfortable. Even when we have nothing left to give. There will never be a time when we regret doing.

And finally, she would tell you to stop asking for permission. To stop waiting for perfect. To stop looking for a sign. But if you absolutely needed one, she would be there, cheering you on and encouraging you to **JUST DO!**

ACKNOWLEDGEMENTS

This may be the most challenging part of the book for me to write. Because there simply aren't enough pages, in all the books in the entire world, for me to express my gratitude to all of my people. To all of our people. So I'm going to do my best. But I'm going to fail. I'm going to miss some people. And so I'm sorry if you've felt "missed." Just know, if I missed you, you deserved to be mentioned. And I'm sorry.

Hadley, Cooper, and Macklin - I don't have the words to express how much I love being your daddy. It's my favorite thing in the world. Thanks for putting up with me. Thanks for giving me so much grace. Thanks for loving me so well. And thank you for helping make this book come true. You three and your mommy are the story. I'm just the teller. Thanks for letting me tell.

Mom and Dad (Mimi and Bop) - Y'all are the best parents anyone could ever ask for. I'm just glad that I got to have y'all. Thank you so much for the way that y'all have shown up for us. Not just the last few years. But in all of my years. I love y'all and "thank you" just doesn't seem like enough. I'll be over for a glass of wine tonight and I'll tell y'all in person how grateful I am. And tomorrow night. And the next. And every night. For the rest of your lives. We are gonna need more wine. Love y'all so much.

Debi and Larry (Grandma and Papa) - Thank you for molding Rachel into the girl that I fell in love with. Thank you for allowing me to have her hand in marriage. Thank you for always showing up. From the time Rachel was a little one, to today, y'all have always shown up. It's pretty clear to me where Rachel learned how to love people so well. It was by watching the two of you. Thank you for continuing to be such a positive and encouraging presence in Hadley, Cooper, and Macklin's lives. We love doing life with y'all. Our door is always open, please keep showing up. Just like Rachel would.

Brian and Kim - Again, I just don't have the right words. From "The 39" to today, y'all were just there. Even from 3,000 miles away, with 5 kids of your own, you always showed up. In the hardest of hards and in the greatest of greats, y'all just did. I love so much that I get to have y'all as my people. Thank you doesn't seem to say enough for how grateful I am for you two.

Taylor and Mike - Thank you guys for stepping up the way you did when Rach was sick and thank you for stepping in the way y'all have since she's been gone. I know none of it's been easy, but y'all have showed up so well. T, I've probably never said this, but I'm proud of you and I'm kinda glad you're my sister. Coach Mike, thank you for marrying Taylor. And for grabbing that beer with me that one time.

RJ - Man. It doesn't matter what I have to say, what matters is what Rach would say. And she'd not only say thank you but she'd be so dang proud of the way you've shown up for me and the kids. You're making her proud bro. And I'm not sure anything I could say means more than that. Love you homie. Cheers 2 Rach.

Molly and Morgan - Thank you for being there for so much of "The 39" and all the days that have followed. Morgan, I'm sorry your book wasn't received as well as mine. I think this may just prove once in for all Mizzou > Harvard. Tacos and Ritas soon? On me this time. Gosh I love y'all.

Aunt Holly and Uncle Frank - Man did she love y'all. You were her home away from home and I know that she'd do anything for just one more hug from the two of you. Thank you for loving my girl so well. For taking care of her when she was under your roof and for opening up your lives and allowing me in.

Tim - Thank you for making these words that I'd written into a book. A real, live, book. There is not a chance in the world that this comes together without you. I can't believe we actually did it! But I need you to stop crying now. We have another book to write. Just Do 2? Just Do, Again? Either way, I'm looking forward to it buddy.

Heather - I know you miss her so much but I hope you know that she misses you too. Thank you for always being that voice in my head reminding me that she'd be proud of me. Even on my worst days, you continue to be that voice. Thank you. And for what it's worth, she'd be so dang proud of you too.

Ashley and Adam - Showing up is an understatement. Y'all take it to another level. And it's beautiful. Thank you for loving us so well. Even if we hate the color orange and can't stand the "Vowels." Gosh, we love y'all and are so thankful you're in our lives.

Tiffany - Thanks for continuing to invite me to everything, even though I've never shown up. And for always supporting us, no matter what that may look like. You just keep doing. I know we are getting expensive. I'm just glad you're rich. Love you friend.

Big B - Thanks for bringing me to Hawaii with you. Without Hawaii, I don't think I would have won the girl. So without you, there would have been no us. And that would suck. So thank you. And of course Becky too. Go Big Red.

Karthi - Thanks for asking me, "Hey man, do you play volleyball?" And then for being my friend because I said that I did. I still wonder if we'd be cool if I hadn't said "yes." You've always been there for me and you were always Rachel's favorite Indian. Congrats on that. That's a big deal.

FP - You just keep showing up. I've tried to get rid of you but it's impossible. So I give up. Thanks for being my wingman for the past 20 years. We may as well try for another 20? Oh and Go Astros.

Andy, Jeff, and David - I love doing business stuff with y'all but it's the life stuff that's much more fun. Appreciate you guys being by our side in the good times and the really hard ones as well. I'm not sure where we'd be today without y'all showing up the way you did. Love you guys.

Hannah and Alexa - You already know. But just in case you didn't read the book and skipped to this. Thank you for stepping into our messy lives and loving us all so well despite it.

Jeremy - Thanks for taking part in the book, for writing the foreword, and for doing your part to help make this project come to life. But more than that, thanks for not only being a great friend to me but also for being Mack's best buddy in the whole wide world. Well, Snoop and then you. But 2nd to Snoop ain't that bad.

Josh, Matt, & Ryan - Thanks for always being willing to take out your mom's credit card to sign up for whatever it is that I pitch y'all. You'll always be my first three calls because I know that I can count on y'all to answer. Good, bad, or ugly. Thanks for always answering my call. Love you broskis.

Courtney - Thank you for making my words not suck as bad and for going to that high school dance with me. They were both equally as important at the time that they took place. Oh, and Chris is so proud of you. I know it.

Nick - You're the ultimate shower-upper. From the hospital room to the living room. You just show up. With your time. With your treasure. With your talent. Thank you for always showing up and thank you for encouraging me to do the same. Love you brother.

The Boys at ORCC - I know that most of y'all can't read. But maybe you'll catch the audio or have your wives read it out loud to you. That being said, thank you guys so much for welcoming pops and me into your community. You guys are some of the good ones.

Chance - I'm so glad you keep getting marked safe. Because if one day you weren't I'm not sure who'd push me to get things done. Just like this book. Thanks for the push.

Pastor Rick - Thank you for showing up and for giving me permission to be relieved. And for fulfilling the promise you made to Rachel to keep showing up for the kids and me. Go, Cubs, Go.

Chandler, Rachel, Brooke, Kim, Cat, Kirsten, and all of the other nurses that made our 39 nights at Parkwest Hospital much more comfortable than it should have been. Thank you all so much for having "her" and for loving us all so well.

Dr. Robinson, Dr. Wheeler, Dr. Brandon, Dr. McHam, and all the other doctors that took part in keeping Rachel alive and then keeping her comfortable. Thank you. And at the same time, I bet Rachel would say, "You're welcome." You're welcome for getting to take care of such an incredible person.

Mrs. Malone, Mrs. Golden, Mrs. Smith, Mrs. Goebel. Ms. Mattson, Mrs. Stephens, Mrs. Church, Mrs. Williams, Dr. Scheafnocker, Mr. Tim, and all the other teachers and staff at Hardin Valley Elementary and Cavett Elementary - Thank you all for watching over my kids from 6:49 am - 2:52 p.m. each day. But more than that, thank you for loving them all the hours of all the days. Whether they are with you or not, y'all just keep showing up.

The State of Nebraska and all the people that claim it as their own - I've got nothing but love for y'all. Sorry I bashed you a little bit. But I wouldn't trade our time there and getting to know all of you for anything in the world. Except for Hawaii or Florida or Texas or really anywhere else that's not cold all the dang time.

All my widowed friends - You know who you are and you know how much you mean to me. I hate the circumstances that brought us together but I sure do love the heck out of y'all and am so glad I get to know all of you. Thank you for holding space with me and for allowing me into yours. Thank you for your willingness to hang with me in my pain. Just a little reminder today, you're not alone. I'm with you.

To those of you who showed up when we first got diagnosed. To all of you that showed up during our 39. And to the so many of you who keep showing up to this very day. Thank you. You know who you are and I'm so sorry if I ever missed saying thank you. But this is me doing that. Thank you.

To those who helped make this book come to life. Whether that was through pledging, sharing or praying. I can't thank y'all enough. I still can't even believe that of all the books in the world, you took the time to read this one. To read my book. Y'all are the real MVPs.

KEEP UP WITH BRANDON AND THE KIDS!

JOIN BRANDON'S COMMUNITY:

Text
JUSTDO to
(865) 326-3065

- AND -

FOLLOW HIM AT:

📷 @brandonjanous
f @brandon.janous

Check out
BRANDONJANOUS.COM
for all the latest news and information!

BRING BRANDON TO YOUR EVENT!
Request information on live appearances at **BrandonJanous.com**

JUST DO! book and audio available at **BrandonJanous.com**